KV-029-229

PELICAN BOOKS

EDITED BY V. K. KRISHNA MENON

Advisory Editors : H. L. BEALES, Reader in Economic
History, University of London; W. E. WILLIAMS,
Secretary, the British Institute of Adult Education;
SIR PETER CHALMERS-MITCHELL, C.B.E., F.R.S., F.Z.S.,
DR.SC., LL.D., Secretary of the Zoological Society
1903—1935

UR OF THE CHALDEES

BY C. LEONARD WOOLLEY

PELICAN BOOKS

UR OF THE CHALDEES

A Record of Seven Years of Excavation

BY

C. LEONARD WOOLLEY

*Director of the Joint Expedition of the British
Museum and the Museum of the University
of Pennsylvania to Mesopotamia*

ILLUSTRATED

PUBLISHED BY
PENGUIN BOOKS LIMITED
HARMONDSWORTH MIDDLESEX ENGLAND

First Published DECEMBER 1929
Second Impression DECEMBER 1929
Third Impression DECEMBER 1929
Fourth Impression JANUARY 1930
Fifth Impression APRIL 1930
Sixth Impression OCTOBER 1930
Seventh Impression OCTOBER 1931
Eighth Impression MARCH 1935
Published in Pelican Books 1938

MADE AND PRINTED IN GREAT BRITAIN FOR PENGUIN BOOKS LIMITED
BY PURNELL AND SONS, LTD., PAULTON (SOMERSET) AND LONDON

CONTENTS

LIST OF ILLUSTRATIONS

Between pages 64–65

MAPS

FOREWORD

In this book I have attempted to describe in a popular form the work which during the last seven years has been done at Ur by the Joint Expedition of the British Museum and the Museum of the University of Pennsylvania. The results of the excavations have aroused very general interest, and it is in answer to requests from many quarters that I have undertaken this account.

The final publication of the results of such an expedition as this is necessarily a slow matter: one volume, that on al 'Ubaid, has already appeared, but some time must pass before other volumes are prepared for the Press. In the meantime there is a widespread desire for information. The annual reports are not accessible to everyone and are often too detailed for general readers, and newspaper accounts dealing with successive phases of the work are ephemeral and even in the mass give no connected picture. In my book *The Sumerians* I illustrated freely from our discoveries the history and achievements of the race now resuscitated from oblivion, but of the actual work of the expedition as carried on and of its results there has been no consecutive story told. This gap I have here tried to fill; and though this small book does not in any way anticipate the official publications which will ultimately appear, does not in fact contain nearly all the material which has already figured in the reports in the *Antiquaries' Journal*, it may yet meet the needs of those who are interested in what the Expedition has already done and wish to follow with better understanding its future discoveries.

Rough Map showing the position of Ur in Sumeria.

INTRODUCTION

Ur lies about half-way between Baghdad and the head of the Persian Gulf, some ten miles west of the present course of the Euphrates. A mile and a half to the east of the ruins runs the single line of railway which joins Basra to the capital of Iraq, and between the rail and the river there is sparse cultivation and little villages of mud huts or reed-mat shelters are dotted here and there; but westwards of the line is desert blank and unredeemed. Out of this waste rise the mounds which were Ur, called by the Arabs after the highest of them all, the Ziggurat hill, 'Tel al Muqayyar,' the Mound of Pitch.

Standing on the summit of this mound one can distinguish along the eastern skyline the dark tasselled fringe of the palm-gardens on the river's bank, but to north and west and south as far as the eye can see stretches a waste of unprofitable sand. To the south-west the flat line of the horizon is broken by a grey upstanding pinnacle, the ruins of the staged tower of the sacred city of Eridu which the Sumerians believed to be the oldest city upon earth, and to the north-west a shadow thrown by the low sun may tell the where-abouts of the low mound of al 'Ubaid; but otherwise nothing relieves the monotony of the vast plain over which the shimmering heat-waves dance and the mirage spreads its mockery of placid waters. It seems incredible that such a wilderness should ever have been habitable for man, and yet the weathered hillocks at one's feet cover the temples and houses of a very great city.

As long ago as 1854 Mr. J. E. Taylor, British Consul at Basra, was employed by the British Museum to investigate some of the southern sites of Mesopotamia, and chose for his chief work the Mound of Pitch. Here he unearthed inscriptions which for the first time revealed that the nameless ruin was none other than Ur, so-called 'of the Chaldees,' the home of Abraham. Taylor's discoveries were not at the time apprised at their true worth and his excavations closed down after two seasons; but more and more the importance of the site came to be recognised, and though, partly through lack of funds and partly because of the lawless character of the district into which foreigners could penetrate only at their own risk, no further excavations were undertaken, yet the British Museum never gave up hope of carrying on the work which Taylor had begun.

Towards the end of the nineteenth century an expedition sent out by the University of Pennsylvania visited Ur and contrived to do a little excavation of which the results have never been published, and then again the site lay fallow until the Great War brought British troops into Mesopotamia and gave an opportunity for long-cherished hopes to be revived and realised. In 1918 Mr. R. Campbell Thompson, formerly assistant in the British Museum and then on the Intelligence Staff of the Army in Mesopotamia, excavated at Eridu and made soundings at Ur. The British Museum was encouraged to put a regular expedition into the field, and when Mr. Leonard King, who was to have led it, fell ill, Dr. H. R. Hall took his place and during the winter of 1918–19 dug at Ur, Eridu, and al 'Ubaid. Dr. Hall's work at Ur was of an experimental nature, richer in promise than fulfilment, but his expedition was of prime importance in that he discovered and partly excavated the little mound of al 'Ubaid with its remarkable remains of early architectural decoration.

Again the want of pence which vexes public institutions brought matters to a standstill. Then, in 1922, Dr. G. B. Gordon, Director of the University Museum of Pennsylvania, approached the British Museum with the proposal of a joint expedition to Mesopotamia; the offer was accepted, and Ur was chosen as the scene of operations. The directorship of the Joint Expedition was entrusted to me, and now for seven winters in succession work has been carried on in the field, with what success this book is meant to show.

UR OF THE CHALDEES

CHAPTER I

THE BEGINNINGS OF UR, AND THE FLOOD

THE history of Ur goes back far beyond the Flood into those dim days when the Euphrates Valley, at least at its lower end, was still a great marsh through which the waters of the two rivers made their sluggish way to the sea. Gradually, as the streams brought down more and more silt from the north, the marsh land began to shrink, 'the waters were gathered together into one place, and the dry land appeared,' and from the uplands of Arabia or from the higher reaches of the middle Euphrates settlers drifted down to occupy such islands as gave a chance for men to live and cultivate the earth, that rich alluvial soil which as soon as it was free from the water would 'bring forth grass, the herb yielding seed, and the fruit tree yielding fruit after his kind, whose seed is in itself.'

One of these islands was Ur. Our excavations have not yet gone deep enough to lay bare more than a few scattered relics of the very early days, but at al 'Ubaid, about four miles from Ur, we have dug out part of such a primitive settlement. Here a little knoll, fortunately never covered afterwards with buildings, preserved the remains of huts constructed of mud and wattle or slight timber framing filled in with reed mats, with floors of beaten mud and fireplaces of mud or crude brick, and wooden doors whose hinge-poles turned on stone sockets.

In the ruins we found quantities of the fine painted hand-made pottery such as occurs in the lowest levels touched at Ur (Plate I *a*), rougher household wares used for cooking and storage, hoes and adzes of chipped and polished stone, saw-toothed flints and flakes of imported volcanic glass, sickles made of hard-baked clay (Plate I *b*), all the evidence of a very simple culture. It was clear that these people cultivated the soil and reaped their harvest of grain; they kept domesticated cattle, sheep and goats; they fished in the marshes (for we found fish-hooks and model boats), and, judging from fragments of painted terra-cotta figures of men and women, they seem to have painted or tatooed their bodies; stone weights showed that the loom was known, so that they had advanced beyond the stage when men wore only the skins of beasts (though the tradition of such sheep-skin garments remained on into much later times); and for luxury they had beads cut from shell or rudely chipped from transparent white quartz, carnelian, and obsidian.

There was nothing to show to what race these first inhabitants of Mesopotamia belonged, but it is natural to connect them with the Semitic-speaking Akkadians whom later on we find occupying the northern half of the river-valley; in any case we can see them as a primitive, not to say a barbarous people who, while they had certainly made some advance on the road to civilisation, were yet very far from being what we should term a civilised community.

At al 'Ubaid the settlement seems to have been comparatively short-lived; at Ur a similar settlement but on a much larger scale must have endured for a very long time; and as the frail mud huts fell into decay and over the ruins of them new huts were built, only to collapse and be built over in their turn, the ground-level rose, just as it does in any modern mud-built village of the Near East, and what had been a low island became a hill. Then, at a date which we cannot fix, people of a new race made their way into the valley, coming whence we do not know, and settled down side by side with the old inhabitants. These were the Sumerians.

Quoting probably some legend of the Sumerians themselves, the Old Testament says that 'the people journeyed from the East and came into the plain of Shinar' (which is Babylon), 'and dwelt there,' and of recent years excavations so far away to the east as the valley of the Indus river have produced remains of an early civilisation which has certain elements in common with what we find in Mesopotamia. The Sumerians believed that they came into the country with their civilisation already formed, bringing with them the knowledge of agriculture, of working in metal, of the art of writing—'since then,' said they, 'no new inventions have been made'—and if, as our excavations seem to show, there is a good deal of truth in that tradition, then it was not in the Euphrates valley that the arts were born, and though it is not likely to have been the Indus valley either, later research may well discover some site between those two extremes where the ancestors of our Sumerians developed the first real civilisation of which we have any knowledge.

At Ur, as elsewhere, the newcomers took over the old hill-village and rebuilt it as a town, putting up permanent buildings of burnt brick and surrounding it with stout walls of defence. The former inhabitants were not driven out, but, inferior as they were in all the arts of life, must have sunk to the condition of serfs. In the lowest levels which we have yet excavated we find their handiwork mixed up with that of the Sumerians, the old painted pottery side by side with the wheel-made clay pots and stone vessels of the higher civilisation, so that we can safely argue for a mixed population; but just as the Norman castle from its hills dominated the low-lying village of the English villeins, so must we suppose that here the walled town

was more or less reserved for the moral conquerors
of the country, the Sumerians, while the 'barbarians'
put up their mud huts at the foot of the mound's slope
or on the flat cultivated land. Many generations passed:
the acropolis of Ur rose higher and higher into the
air as the refuse of its houses was piled in the streets
or flung out over its walls—and then came the Flood.

It has long been agreed that the story of the Flood
as told in Genesis is based on the Sumerian legend,
of which the oldest written versions that we possess
go back more than two thousand years before Christ
and are therefore some centuries older than Abraham,
but many authorities have doubted whether either
story had any basis in historical fact. That the Sumerians
had no such doubt is clear, for, apart from the legend,
overlaid as it is with mythology and miracle, the annalists
in their sober table of the reigns of kings made mention
of it as an event which interrupted the course of history:
they vouchsafe us no details about it—'then came the
Flood, and after the Flood kingship again descended
from heaven'—but since two or three Sumerian cities
are said to have existed equally before the Deluge and
after it, we may assume that the historical break was not
final, and that so far from the disaster being universal
some at least of the local centres of civilisation survived
it. Fuller references to the Flood may yet be discovered
on tablets buried in the fertile soil of Mesopotamia,
but even then some might doubt whether these did
more than amplify a legend: the historian is apt to
demand material proof, and material proof of such
an event as this is very hard to find.

During the seasons 1927–8 and 1928–9 our work on
the prehistoric graveyard had resulted in the excavation
of a huge pit some 200 feet across and between 30 and
40 feet deep. Now, practically the whole of the soil
which we had removed consisted of household rubbish
—the grey ashes from hearth fires, black soot, and

half-burnt wood, grey mud bricks decomposed and
returned to their original clay, burnt bricks broken or
by the action of organic salts reduced to red and yellow
dust, masses of potsherds, all in well-defined layers
sloping steeply down in one direction with holes and
pockets here and there which scarcely interrupted the
remarkable uniformity of the strata in general. At the
south-west end, where the ground rises to a high mound,
the slope of the rubbish-layers was more pronounced
and the more sharp the deeper we dug; to the north-
east there was a gentler run, the strata getting thicker
as they went deeper, and low down they became quite
horizontal, and the sherds of pottery which elsewhere
had lain at all angles were here flat and massed at the
bottom of each layer, while the soil in which they lay
was smooth as if water-laid and faded off at the top
of each stratum to a muddy black. It was into this
rubbish that the royal and other graves had been dug,
and the rubbish extended down below the graves.

There was only one explanation which would meet
the case. The rubbish was of course older, probably
much older, than the royal graves dug down into it,
ancient as they were; the slope of the strata showed
that it was not the rubbish which accumulates in an
inhabited spot, for there the layers would lie horizontally, but had been thrown out as refuse, and it had
been thrown out from a height situated at the south-
west end of our excavation. The only height from which
refuse could so be thrown was the wall, or the buildings,
of the early town: the first rubbish would be heaped
against the wall; what was emptied over this would
run down and form a talus, its slope growing less steep
as the foot of the pile spread farther out; with the rise
in the level of the town itself the mound too would rise,
but always it would stretch farther afield, and at last
people would be unable to pour out their refuse from
the wall, because the slope of the mound would be too

gradual for it to run down, and would be obliged to
carry it out and dump it on the mound's face: this
would account for the flattened layers at the north-
east end; and the muddy strata with the pottery lying
horizontally proved that the rubbish mound ended in
a water-channel running parallel with the town walls.
Led on by this, we made soundings beyond the south
west end of our trench and found the walls and floors
of the primitive town.

Rubbish mounds 40 feet high must represent a long
period of time, a period certainly to be reckoned in
centuries, and with the excavation of the lowest graves
we were not yet at the bottom of the rubbish. In the
early spring of 1929, in the hopes of getting some
chronological evidence, we began sinking shafts below
the level of the deepest graves. Almost at once discoveries were made which confirmed our previous views,
if such confirmation were necessary: just below the
floor of one of the royal tombs, in a layer of burnt
wood ash, there were found numerous clay tablets
inscribed with characters of a much more archaic type
than those of the inscriptions in the graves. The discovery was made at the north-east end of the excavated
area, where even the lowest rubbish would belong to
a comparatively late period in the formation of the
mound; but as on the evidence of the writing the tablets
might be assigned to about the thirty-seventh century
before Christ—were, that is, two or three hundred
years older than the tombs—we had a satisfactory
chronology for this particular stratum, and of course
the farther we dug at the same level towards the south-
west the older would be the material we should encounter.

One point struck us as most important. However
deep we dug into the rubbish and however much our
work carried us back in time behind the period of the
royal graves, the objects found in that rubbish, pottery
and the like, were precisely the same as what was

found in the tombs themselves. In other words, throughout the whole period represented by the growth of the
refuse dumps (so far as we had penetrated into them)
and by the early cemetery the material civilisation of
the people, at least on its domestic side, had changed
remarkably little; such variations as we found, in the
writing for instance, meant no more than the development which is to be expected in the course of centuries,
but development along uniform lines by people of the
same race. The wonderful civilisation illustrated by
the contents of the graves, which I shall describe later,
had always seemed to imply a long past behind it;
now we had proof of just such a steady growth as we
had assumed.

The shafts went deeper, and suddenly the character
of the soil changed. Instead of the stratified pottery
and rubbish we were in perfectly clean clay, uniform
throughout, the texture of which showed that it had
been laid there by water. The workmen declared that
we had come to the bottom of everything, to the river
silt of which the original delta was formed, and at
first, looking at the sides of the shaft, I was disposed
to agree with them, but then I saw that we were too
high up. It was difficult to believe that the island on
which the first settlement was built stood up so much
above what must have been the level of the marsh,
and after working out the measurements I sent the
men back to work to deepen the hole. The clean clay
continued without change—the sole object found in it
was a fragment of fossilised bone which must have
been brought down with the clay from the upper reaches
of the river—until it had attained a thickness of a
little over 8 feet. Then, as suddenly as it had begun,
it stopped, and we were once more in layers of rubbish
full of stone implements, flint cores from which the
implements had been flaked off, and pottery.

But here there was a remarkable change. Some of

the pottery was exactly like what we had been finding
above the clay and in the tombs, but mixed with this
there were bits of the hand-made painted ware which
distinguishes the pre-Sumerian village of al 'Ubaid,
while the numerous flint implements, which evidently
were being manufactured on the spot, were similar to
those from al 'Ubaid and further differentiated this
from the higher strata where flints were very rarely
to be found. The great bed of clay marked, if it did
not cause, a break in the continuity of history: above
it we had the pure Sumerian civilisation slowly developing on its own lines; below it there was a mixed culture
of which one element was Sumerian and the other
of that al 'Ubaid type which seems to have nothing
to do with the Sumerians but to belong to the race
which inhabited the river-valley before the Sumerians
came into it.

One object which lay with the flints and potsherds
under the clay was of prime importance. It was a
brick of burnt clay. Now, the ruins which we had
previously excavated at Ur cover a period of more
than two thousand five hundred years, and at every
age when there was much building activity the type of
brick employed shows some modification; the standards
of measure, the relative proportions of the bricks,
change, often different clays are used, and one can
generally recognise at a glance and nearly always con-
firm with a metre scale the date of any wall or isolated
brick. But this brick was different from any we had
ever seen. Certainly it belonged to a period of which
we had had no experience hitherto, and in a curious
way it gave the impression of being older than any
brick we had seen; but what it did conclusively prove
was that in this age of mixed culture Ur was not like
al 'Ubaid, a village of mud huts and reed shelters,
but contained permanent buildings solidly constructed,
the town of a civilised people.

We had long before this seen the meaning of our discovery. The bed of water-laid clay deposited against the sloping face of the mound, which extended from the town to the stream or canal at the north-east end, could only have been the result of a flood; no other agency could possibly account for it. Inundations are of normal occurrence in Lower Mesopotamia, but no ordinary rising of the rivers would leave behind it anything approaching the bulk of this clay bank: 8 feet of sediment imply a very great depth of water, and the flood which deposited it must have been of a magnitude unparalleled in local history. That it was so is further proved by the fact that the clay bank marks a definite break in the continuity of the local culture; a whole civilisation which existed before it is lacking above it and seems to have been submerged by the waters.

Taking into consideration all the facts, there could be no doubt that the flood of which we had thus found the only possible evidence was the Flood of Sumerian history and legend, the Flood on which is based the story of Noah. A pit sunk 300 yards away to the north-west gave us the same bed of water-laid clay, with beneath it the same flints and coloured pottery of the non-Sumerian folk; the next step was to test the higher part of the ancient town mound above the level which the clay formed as the receding waters deposited it against the mound's bank.

Time was short and only a small area could be excavated, and that not to a depth which could be expected to yield cultural remains of the al 'Ubaid type unmixed with those of the later comers. But going down through successive levels of occupation marked by floors of burnt brick or of beaten mud lying one above the other and by the ruins of house walls, we did pass quite suddenly from strata containing nothing but purely Sumerian remains to others which yielded side by side with these the familiar painted clay pots and implements of flint and volcanic glass; and tracing downhill the sloping layers of the rubbish we were able to prove that these mixed levels in the town site corresponded to the rubbish layers which underlay the clay bank: about sixteen feet below a brick pavement which we could with tolerable certainty date as being not later than 3200 B.C., we were down in the ruins of that Ur which existed before the Flood.

Work on a much larger scale must be done before we shall be able to describe in any detail the culture of the antediluvian age; at present we have done little more than prove its existence. One point, however, deserves to be emphasised: in the ruins of the houses we have found numerous lumps of hard clay which had been the stoppers of bottles or jars, and stamped on these were the impressions of the owners' seals; there were no inscriptions, but designs sometimes of an elaborate geometrical character, sometimes with rows of animals shown walking in hilly country, the figures drawn with an astonishing liveliness and skill. It is probable that where seals were employed the art of writing was already known, so that we may not unreasonably hope to unearth written documents actually older than the Flood; but in any case the carving of these seals with their combination of naturalism with formed style bespeaks a state of society well advanced on the road to civilisation properly so called.

So much for the facts. What, then, is to be built up on them? The discovery that there was a real deluge to which the Sumerian and the Hebrew stories of the Flood alike go back does not of course prove any single detail in either of those stories. This deluge was not universal, but a local disaster confined to the lower valley of the Tigris and Euphrates, affecting an area perhaps 400 miles long and 100 miles across; but for the occupants of the valley that was the whole world !

I have said that in all probability of the two races which inhabited together the lower valley the Sumerians were the city dwellers and the non-Sumerians lived in such open and low-lying villages as we found at al 'Ubaid: a flood great enough to account for the eight-foot bank of clay would certainly have drowned out those mud-hut villages; it is conceivable that it might spare some at least of the Sumerian cities, perched high on their mounds and protected by walls of burnt brick.

According to Sumerian annals, some of the cities did survive; and though Ur is not mentioned amongst them, the fact that it lay so high and the discovery of burnt brick in its ruins makes its survival quite possible. In this way we can explain what before was one of the great puzzles of South Mesopotamian archæology, the sudden and complete disappearance of the painted pottery which at one time seems to have been universally distributed over the southern sites. The people who made it, the older inhabitants of the country, were wiped out by the Flood, and the Sumerians who survived it were able not only to develop their own civilisation uncontaminated, as our excavations prove they did, but also to advance northward and occupy the empty lands, with the result that they who according to their own tradition, were originally but settlers on the sea-coast of the Persian Gulf, are found when history opens to be masters of the delta for a distance of 200 miles from the sea.

Plan of Ur.

CHAPTER II

THE GRAVES OF THE KINGS OF UR

I HAVE said that the discovery of the evidence of the Flood was a result of the excavation of the royal tombs. The greater part of three seasons' work has been devoted to the clearing of the great cemetery which lay outside the walls of the old town and occupied the rubbish heaps piled up between them and the water-channel, and the treasures which have been unearthed from the graves during that time have revolutionised our ideas of the early civilisation of the world.

The cemetery (there are really two cemeteries, one above the other, but I am speaking now only of the lower and older) consists of burials of two sorts, the graves of commoners and the tombs of kings. Because the latter have yielded the richest works of art one is inclined to think of them alone, but the graves of the common folk, as well as being a hundred-fold as many in number, have also produced very fine objects, and have afforded precious evidence for the dating of the cemetery.

The tombs of the kings appear to be on the whole earlier in date than the graves of their subjects, and this is not so much because they lie at a deeper level, for that might be explained as a natural precaution, the larger and richer graves being dug deeper as a protection against robbers, but because of their relative positions. It is a common sight to see in a Moslem graveyard the tomb of some local saint surmounted by its little domed chapel and the other graves crowded round this as close as may be, as if the occupants sought the protection of the holy man. So it is with the royal tombs at Ur. The older private graves are clustered

round them, bordering on them but respecting their
sanctity; later it seems as if the visible monuments
of the dead kings vanished and their memory faded,
leaving only a vague tradition of this being holy ground,
and we find the newer graves invading the shafts of
the royal tombs and dug right down into them.

The private graves are found at very varying levels,
partly perhaps because there was no regular standard of
depth, partly because the ground surface of the cemetery
was far from uniform; but, generally speaking, the higher
graves are the later, and this is due to the rise in the
ground-level, which went on steadily throughout the
time that the graveyard was in use. The result of this
rise obliterating the position of the older graves was
that a new grave might be placed directly above an old
but, being started from a higher level, would not go
quite so far down, and we may find as many as half a
dozen graves superimposed one above the other. When
this is so, the position in the ground necessarily corres-
ponds to the order in time, and from these superimposed
graves we get most valuable evidence for chronology.

Judging from the character of their contents, pottery,
etc., the later graves seem to come just before the
beginning of the First Dynasty of Ur (*vide* Chapter
III), which we date to about 3100 B.C., and a few are
actually contemporary with that dynasty; for the
cemetery age as a whole I think that we must allow a
period of at least 300 years. The first of the royal tombs
then, may be dated soon after 3500 B.C., and soon after
3200 B.C. the graveyard was falling out of use. There
is not space here to go into all the arguments, but
everyone, I think, will agree that some time must have
elapsed before the kings, buried as they were with such
ghastly pomp, could be forgotten and the sanctity
of the tomb-shafts be invaded by the common dead;
and if we find above them six or more superimposed
burials, between each of which there must have been

a decent lapse of time, and the topmost of these dates before 3100 B.C., then the chronology which I suggest will not seem exaggeratedly long.

Often the first sign that the workmen have of a grave as they dig down into the mixed soil of the cemetery is a paper-thin wavy line of white powder or else a few small holes set in a line and running vertically into the earth; either of these means the abandonment of pick and spade and the careful use of excavating knives. The holes are left by the decay of the wooden staves which strengthened the sides of a wooden or wickerwork coffin, the wavy white line is the edge of the reed mat which lined the grave or in which the bodies of poorer folk were wrapped. It is an astonishing thing that in soil wherein so much that seems enduring decays entirely, a fragile thing like a piece of matting, though it lose all its substance and can be blown away with a breath, yet retains its appearance and its texture and can with care be exposed in such condition that a photograph of it looks like one of the real matting which perished 5,000 years ago. So too with wood; nothing of it survives, but on the soil there is left an impression, a cast as it were, which with its effect of grain and colour might deceive the eye, though a touch of the finger obliterates it more easily than it dislodges the plumage from the wing of a butterfly.

The ordinary grave consisted of a rectangular pit; at the bottom of this the body might be laid wrapped up in a roll of matting secured by a long copper pin; or the dead man might be placed in a coffin, usually of wood or wickerwork, sometimes of clay. In either case we find with the body such personal belongings as beads and ear-rings, a knife or dagger, the pins that fastened the dress, and perhaps the cylinder seal the impression of which on a clay tablet was equivalent to the owner's signature. Outside the coffin or the matting roll were set what were more properly offerings to the dead, food and drink in vessels of clay, copper, or stone, weapons and tools; in most cases mats lined the bottom of the pit and were laid over the offerings to keep them from immediate contact with the earth which was thrown back to fill the grave. The body lies always on its side, the legs slightly bent at hip and knee in the attitude of one asleep, and the hands are brought up before the face and hold close to the mouth a cup which must once have contained water. There does not seem to be any fixed rule for the direction of the body, no such orientation as is practised in Christian and Moslem lands to-day, and the graves often lie at right angles with their neighbours; only the attitude of the body in the grave is constant.

The provision made for the dead seems clearly to prove a belief in a future life of some sort, but there is nothing found which expressly defines such belief; in no single grave has there been any figure of a god, any symbol or ornament that strikes one as being of a religious nature; the dead man took with him what he might require for a journey to or for a sojourn in another world, but what he thought about the world to which he was going nothing tells us. On the other hand, the material life of the people is illustrated to a wonderful degree by the contents of their graves, and even had there been no royal tombs with their wealth of artistic treasures, we should have been able to obtain from the cemetery a very detailed knowledge of the civilisation of the age.

As we are dealing here with a period of which previously nothing was known, every object is in the nature of an historic monument, and a poor grave may contain something which while not intrinsically valuable is historically most precious. Thus last winter there was found standing by the side of a clay coffin robbed in antiquity and empty a painted clay vase of a type which had never before occurred in the whole of our cemetery work or indeed in the course of our excavations at Ur. Unique here, it would have been thoroughly at home in the prehistoric levels at Susa, far away in Persia, and being found where it was proved some intercourse between Persia and Ur towards the close of the cemetery period; either some Persian immigrant had been buried here or the native owner of the imported vase had determined to take it with him to the grave.

As soon as a grave is detected, the workman concerned reports to the foreman and is instructed how to proceed. The first objects to be exposed are usually the clay pots, because these, if not crushed by the weight of the earth, stand higher than the other objects in the pit's bottom. Next the position of the body has to be ascertained—not always an easy matter, since the bones are often so decayed that only a difference in the colour of the soil betrays their presence; and then the outline of the original grave-shaft is traced and the earth gradually removed from its whole area, only that round and over the head being left, as here if anywhere the more precious objects will be found. If anything of importance appears, gold or silver or beads, the workman must again stop work and report, and then one of the staff takes over the task of excavation. Nothing must be disturbed until the grave has been finally cleared, written up, drawn and photographed if necessary; beads, if there are any, have to be noted in such wise that they can be re-strung in their original order, so as to reproduce the fashion of the time; the skull, should it chance to be unusually well preserved, has to be treated with hot paraffin wax and removed for study at home; the position of the grave is recorded on the plan; and then, when nothing of it is left, pick and spade start again and work is carried down to a deeper level, where more and earlier graves await discovery.

Excavation of this sort is essentially a work of destruction; in the early cemetery and in the cemetery of the Sargonid age which lay immediately above it we have dug and noted more than 1,400 private graves, and in the great yawning pit which is all our work has produced not a vestige of one of these remains, only, at the pit's bottom, the standing masonry of six royal tombs and the outlines, broken and irregular, of the death-pits. All the more care, therefore, must be taken to collect at once all the evidence that a grave may afford, even if its bearing be not immediately clear, for there is no going back later to repair omissions, and on the thoroughness of the note-taking more than on the importance of the objects depends the ultimate value of our work.

The routine of digging private graves may become wearisome, for there is a great deal of repetition and only too many of the graves contain nothing of very obvious interest, though sometimes one is found which by its contents atones for a whole series wherein original poverty or subsequent plundering has disappointed our hopes. More than half the graves have been plundered. During the later part of the time when the cemetery was in use the diggers of the new graves, encountering one of an older day, could not resist the temptation to remove its more valuable contents; at a still later date there was building over the forgotten graveyard, and men employed in making foundations or laying drains made chance discoveries which encouraged them to more deliberate efforts. Sometimes the robbers must have had knowledge of the whereabouts of the tombs of the old kings but feared to attack them openly, for we have found circular shafts driven deep down into the level of the old graves and then turning horizontally to tunnel in the direction of a royal tomb: in some cases they have succeeded all too well; in one or two they missed their mark and abandoned the attempt in disgust; but at Ur, as in Egypt, tomb-robbing is an ancient profession, and we to-day are lucky if we hit upon a grave at once wealthy and intact.

The first of the royal tombs proved a disappointment. At the very end of the season 1926–7 two important discoveries were made. At the bottom of an earth shaft, amongst masses of copper weapons, there was found the famous gold dagger of Ur, a wonderful weapon whose blade was of gold, its hilt of lapis lazuli decorated with gold studs, and its sheath of gold beautifully worked with an openwork pattern derived from plaited grass (Plate IV*b*); with it was another object scarcely less remarkable, a cone-shaped reticule of gold ornamented with a spiral pattern and containing a set of little toilet instruments, tweezers, lancet, and pencil, also of gold. Nothing like these things had ever before come from the soil of Mesopotamia; they revealed an art hitherto unsuspected and they gave promise of future discoveries outstripping all our hopes.

The other discovery was less sensational. Digging down in another part of the cemetery we found what at first appeared to be walls of *terre pisée*, i.e. of earth not moulded into bricks but used as concrete is used for building. As the sun dried the soil and brought out the colours of its stratification, it became evident that these were no built walls but the clean-cut sides of a pit sunk in the rubbish; the looser filling of the pit had fallen away as we worked and had left the original face exactly as the first diggers had made it. As the excavation continued we came on slabs and blocks of rough limestone which seemed to form a paving over the pit's base. This was an astonishing thing, because there is no stone in the Euphrates delta, not so much as a pebble in its alluvium, and to obtain blocks of limestone such as these it is necessary to go some thirty miles away into the higher desert. The cost of transport would be considerable, and the result is that stone is scarcely ever found in buildings at Ur: a stone pavement

B

underground would therefore be an unheard of extravagance. As the season was just at its end we could do no more than clear the surface of the 'pavement' and leave its fuller examination for the next autumn.

Thinking the matter over during the summer, we came to the conclusion that the stones might be not the floor of a building but its roof, and that we might have discovered a royal grave. It was with high hopes that we resumed work in the following autumn and very soon we could assure ourselves that our forecast was correct: we had found a stone-built underground structure which had indeed been the tomb of a king, but a rubbish-filled tunnel led from near the surface to the broken roof, robbers had been there before us, and except for a few scattered fragments of a gold diadem and some decayed copper pots there was nothing left for us to find.

But in spite of that disappointment the discovery was most important. We had laid bare the ruins of a two-chambered structure built of stone throughout with one long and narrow chamber vaulted with stone and a square room which had certainly once been covered with a stone dome, though the collapse of the roof made it difficult to establish the exact method of construction. A doorway, blocked with rubble masonry, afforded entrance to the tomb and was approached by a slanting ramp cut down from the ground surface in the hard soil. Nothing of the sort had ever been found before, and the light thrown on the architectural knowledge of this remote period might well atone for the loss of the tomb's contents; moreover, there was no reason to suppose that this was an isolated tomb, and we could hope for others to which the plunderers had not made their way.

During that season (1927–8) and in the course of last winter more royal tombs came to light, and it is curious to find that never more than two of them are

alike. Two large tombs, both plundered, consist of a
four-roomed building occupying the whole area of the
excavated shaft at the bottom of which they lie; walls
and roofs alike are of limestone rubble, and in each
case there are two long outer chambers which are
vaulted and two smaller central chambers crowned with
domes; a ramp leads to the arched door in the outer
wall, and arched doors give communication between
the rooms. Two graves, those of Queen Shub-ad and
her supposed husband (Plate II), consist of a pit open
to the sky and approached by a sloped ramp, at one
end of which is a single-chamber tomb with limestone
walls and a roof constructed of burnt brick, vaulted and
with apsidal ends; the chamber was destined to receive
the royal body, the open pit was for offerings and subsidiary burials, and was simply filled in with earth.
In another case the pit was found, but the tomb chamber
did not lie inside it, but seems to have been close by
and on a different level. A small grave found last
winter consists of a single stone-built domed chamber
with a little front court at the bottom of the shaft and,
higher up in the shaft, mud-brick buildings for the
subsidiary burials and offerings, the whole being covered
with earth; another has the same general arrangement,
but instead of the domed stone chamber there was a
vaulted chamber of mud brick.

There is variety enough therefore in the actual
structures, but underlying all there was a common
ritual for which different generations provided in
different ways; what that ritual was can best be explained
by describing the excavation of the graves.

In 1927–8, soon after our disappointment with the
plundered stone tomb, we found, in another part of the
field, five bodies lying side by side in a shallow sloping
trench; except for the copper daggers at their waists
and one or two small clay cups they had none of the
normal furniture of a grave, and the mere fact of there

being a number thus together was unusual. Then,
below them, a layer of matting was found, and tracing
this along we came to another group of bodies, those
of ten women carefully arranged in two rows; they
wore head-dresses of gold, lapis lazuli, and carnelian,
and elaborate bead necklaces, but they too possessed
no regular tomb furnishings. At the end of the row lay
the remains of a wonderful harp, the wood of it decayed
but its decoration intact, making its reconstruction only
a matter of care; the upright wooden beam was capped
with gold, and in it were fastened the gold-headed nails
which secured the strings; the sounding-box was edged
with a mosaic in red stone, lapis lazuli and white shell,
and from the front of it projected a splendid head of
a bull wrought in gold with eyes and beard of lapis
lazuli; across the ruins of the harp lay the bones of the
gold-crowned harpist.

By this time we had found the earth sides of the pit
in which the women's bodies lay and could see that the
bodies of the five men were on the ramp which led
down to it. Following the pit along, we came upon
more bones which at first puzzled us by being other
than human, but the meaning of them soon became
clear. A little way inside the entrance to the pit stood
a wooden sledge chariot decorated with red, white, and
blue mosaic along the edges of the framework and with
golden heads of lions having manes of lapis lazuli and
shell on its side panels; along the top rail were smaller
gold heads of lions and bulls, silver lionesses' heads
adorned the front, and the position of the vanished
swingle-bar was shown by a band of blue and white
inlay and two smaller heads of lionesses in silver. In
front of the chariot lay the crushed skeleton of two asses
with the bodies of the grooms by their heads, and on
the top of the bones was the double ring, once attached
to the pole, through which the reins had passed; it
was of silver, and standing on it was a gold 'mascot'

in the form of a donkey most beautifully and realistically modelled.

Close to the chariot were an inlaid gaming-board[1] and a collection of tools and weapons, including a set of chisels and a saw made of gold, big bowls of grey soapstone, copper vessels, a long tube of gold and lapis which was a drinking-tube for sucking up liquor from the bowls, more human bodies, and then the wreckage of a large wooden chest adorned with a figured mosaic in lapis lazuli and shell which was found empty but had perhaps contained such perishable things as clothes. Behind this box were more offerings, masses of vessels in copper, silver, stone (including exquisite examples in volcanic glass, lapis lazuli, alabaster, and marble), and gold (Plate III, b, c); one set of silver vessels seemed to be in the nature of a communion-service, for there was a shallow tray or platter, a jug with tall neck and long spout such as we know from carved stone reliefs to have been used in religious rites, and tall slender silver tumblers nested one inside another; a similar tumbler in gold, fluted and cashed, with a fluted feeding-bowl, a chalice, and a plain oval bowl of gold lay piled together, and two magnificent lions' heads in silver, perhaps the ornaments of a throne, were amongst the treasures in the crowded pit. The perplexing thing was that with all this wealth of objects we had found no body so far distinguished from the rest as to be that of the person to whom all were dedicated; logically our discovery, however great, was incomplete.

The objects were removed and we started to clear away the remains of the wooden box, a chest some 6 feet long and 3 feet across, when under it we found burnt bricks. They were fallen, but at one end some were still in place and formed the ring-vault of a stone

[1] A more elaborate example of a gaming-board is figured on Plate VI b.

chamber. The first and natural supposition was that
here we had the tomb to which all the offerings belonged,
but further search proved that the chamber was plundered,
the roof had not fallen from decay but had been broken
through, and the wooden box had been placed over
the hole as if deliberately to hide it. Then, digging round
the outside of the chamber, we found just such another
pit as that 6 feet above (Plate II). At the foot of the
ramp lay six soldiers, orderly in two ranks, with copper
spears by their sides and copper helmets crushed flat
on the broken skulls; just inside, having evidently been
backed down the slope, were two wooden four-wheeled
waggons each drawn by three oxen—one of the latter
so well preserved that we were able to lift the skeleton
entire; the waggons were plain, but the reins were decorated with long beads of lapis and silver and passed
through silver rings surmounted with mascots in the
form of bulls; the grooms lay at the oxen's heads and
the drivers in the bodies of the cars; of the cars them
selves only the impression of the decayed wood remained
in the soil, but so clear was this that a photograph
showed the grain of the solid wooden wheel and the
grey-white circle which had been the leather tyre.

Against the end wall of the stone chamber lay the
bodies of nine women wearing the gala head-dress of
lapis and carnelian beads from which hung golden
pendants in the form of beech-leaves, great lunate
ear-rings of gold, silver 'combs' like the palm of a hand
with three fingers tipped with flowers whose petals are
inlaid with lapis, gold, and shell, and necklaces of lapis
and gold; their heads were leaned against the masonry,
their bodies extended on to the floor of the pit, and
the whole space between them and the waggons was
crowded with other dead, women and men, while the
passage which led along the side of the chamber to its
arched door was lined with soldiers carrying daggers,
and with women. Of the soldiers in the central space

one had a bundle of four spears with heads of gold, two had sets of four silver spears, and by another there was a remarkable relief in copper with a design of two lions trampling on the bodies of two fallen men which may have been the decoration of a shield.

On the top of the bodies of the 'court ladies' against the chamber wall had been placed a wooden harp, of which there survived only the copper head of a bull and the shell plaques which had adorned the sounding-box; by the side wall of the pit, also set on the top of the bodies, was a second harp with a wonderful bull's head in gold, its eyes, beard, and horn-tips of lapis, and a set of engraved shell plaques not less wonderful; there are four of them with grotesque scenes of animals playing the parts of men, and while the most striking feature about them is that sense of humour which is so rare in ancient art, the grace and balance of the design and the fineness of the drawing make of these plaques one of the most instructive documents that we possess for the appreciation of the art of early Sumer.

Inside the tomb the robbers had left enough to show that it had contained bodies of several minor people as well as that of the chief person, whose name, if we can trust the inscription on a cylinder seal, was A-bar-gi; overlooked against the wall we found two model boats, one of copper now hopelessly decayed, the other of silver wonderfully well preserved (Plate IIIa); some 2 feet long, it has high stern and prow, five seats, and amidships an arched support for the awning which would protect the passenger, and the leaf-bladed oars are still set in the thwarts; it is a testimony to the con-servatism of the East that a boat of identical type is in use to-day on the marshes of the Lower Euphrates, some 50 miles from Ur.

The king's tomb-chamber lay at the far end of his open pit; continuing our search behind it we found a second stone chamber built up against it either at the same time or, more probably, at a later period. This chamber, roofed like the king's with a vault of ring arches in burnt brick, was the tomb of the queen to whom belonged the upper pit with its ass chariot and other offerings: her name, Shub-ad, was given us by a fine cylinder seal of lapis lazuli which was found in the filling of the shaft a little above the roof of the chamber and had probably been thrown into the pit at the moment when the earth was being put back into it. The vault of the chamber had fallen in, but luckily this was due to the weight of earth above, not to the violence of tomb-robbers; the tomb itself was intact (Plate II).

At one end, on the remains of a wooden bier, lay the body of the queen, a gold cup near her hand; the upper part of the body was entirely hidden by a mass of beads of gold, silver, lapis lazuli, carnelian, agate, and chalcedony, long strings of which, hanging from a collar, had formed a cloak reaching to the waist and bordered below with a broad band of tubular beads of lapis, carnelian, and gold: against the right arm were three long gold pins with lapis heads and three amulets in the form of fish, two of gold and one of lapis, and a fourth in the form of two seated gazelles, also of gold.

The head-dress whose remains covered the crushed skull was a more elaborate edition of that worn by the court ladies: its basis was a broad gold ribbon festooned in loops round the hair—and the measurement of the curves showed that this was not the natural hair but a wig padded out to an almost grotesque size; over this came three wreaths, the lowest, hanging down over the forehead, of plain gold ring pendants, the second of beech leaves, the third of long willow leaves in sets of three with gold flowers whose petals were of blue and white inlay; all these were strung on triple chains of lapis and carnelian beads. Fixed into the back of the hair was a golden 'Spanish comb' with five points ending in lapis-centred gold flowers. Heavy spiral rings of gold wire were twisted into the side curls of the wig, huge lunate ear-rings of gold hung down to the shoulders, and apparently from the hair also hung on each side a string of large square stone beads with, at the end of each, a lapis amulet, one shaped as a seated bull and the other as a calf. Complicated as the head-dress was, its different parts lay in such good order that it was possible to reconstruct the whole and exhibit the likeness of the queen with all her original finery in place.

For the purposes of exhibition a plaster cast was made from a well-preserved female skull of the period (the queen's own skull was too fragmentary to be used), and over this my wife modelled the features in wax, making this as thin as possible so as not to obliterate the bone structure; the face was passed by Sir Arthur Keith, who has made a special study of the Ur and al 'Ubaid skulls, as reproducing faithfully the character of the early Sumerians. On this head was put a wig of the correct dimensions dressed in the fashion illustrated by terra-cotta figures which, though later in date, probably represent an old tradition. The gold hair-ribbon had been lifted from the tomb without dis-turbing the arrangement of the strands, these having been first fixed in position by strips of glued paper threaded in and out between them and by wires twisted round the gold; when the wig had been fitted on the head, the hair-ribbon was balanced on the top and the wires and paper bands were cut, and the ribbon fell naturally into place and required no further arranging. The wreaths were re-strung and tied on in the order noted at the time of excavation. Though the face is not an actual portrait of the queen, it gives at least the type to which she must have conformed, and the whole re-constructed head presents us with the most accurate picture we are likely ever to possess of what she looked like in her lifetime.[1]

By the side of the body lay a second head-dress of a novel sort. On to a diadem made apparently of a strip of soft white leather had been sewn thousands of minute lapis lazuli beads, and against this background of solid blue were set a row of exquisitely fashioned gold animals, stags, gazelles, bulls, and goats, with between them clusters of pomegranates, three fruit hanging together shielded by their leaves, and branches of some other tree with golden stems and fruit or pods of gold and carnelian, while gold rosettes were sewn on at intervals, and from the lower border of the diadem hung palmettes of twisted gold wire.

The bodies of two women attendants were crouched against the bier, one at its head and one at its foot, and all about the chamber lay strewn offerings of all sorts, another gold bowl, vessels of silver and copper, stone bowls, and clay jars for food, the head of a cow in silver, two silver tables for offerings, silver lamps, and a number of large cockle-shells containing green paint; such shells are nearly always found in women's graves, and the paint in them presumably used as a cosmetic, may be white, black, or red, but the normal colour is green. Queen Shub-ad's shells were abnormally big, and with them were found two pairs of imitation shells, one in silver and one in gold, each with its green paint.

The discovery was now complete and our earlier difficulty was explained: King A-bar-gi's grave and Queen Shub-ad's were exactly alike, but whereas the former was all on one plane, the queen's tomb-chamber had been sunk below the general level of her grave-pit. Probably they were husband and wife: the king had died first and been buried, and it had been the

[1] This head, with different wig and head-dress, is shown on Plate V.

queen's wish to lie as close to him as might be; for this
end the grave-diggers had reopened the king's shaft,
going down in it until the top of the chamber vault
appeared; then they had stopped work in the main
shaft but had dug down at the back of the chamber
a pit in which the queen's stone tomb could be built.
But the treasures known to lie in the king's grave were
too great a temptation for the workmen; the outer pit
where the bodies of the court ladies lay was protected
by 6 feet of earth which they could not disturb without
being detected, but the richer plunder in the royal
chamber itself was separated from them only by the
bricks of the vault; they broke through the arch, carried
off their spoil, and placed the great clothes-chest of the
queen over the hole to hide their sacrilege.

Nothing else would account for the plundered vault
lying immediately below the untouched grave of the
queen, and the connecting of Shub-ad's stone chamber
with the upper 'death-pit,' as we came to call these
open shafts in which the subsidiary bodies lay, made
an exact parallel to the king's grave and, in a lesser
degree, to the other royal tombs. Clearly, when a royal
person died, he or she was accompanied to the grave
by all the members of the court: the king had at least
three people with him in his chamber and sixty-two in
the death-pit; the queen was content with some twenty-
five in all. Here we had a single stone chamber and an
open death-pit; where there was a larger stone building
with two or four rooms, then one of these was for the
royal body and the rest for the followers sacrificed in
precisely the same way; the ritual was identical, only
the accommodation for the victims differed in different
cases.

On the subject of human sacrifice more light was
thrown by the discovery of a great death-pit excavated
last winter. At about 26 feet below the surface we came
upon a mass of mud brick not truly laid but rammed

together and forming, as we guessed, not a floor but the stopping, as it were, of a shaft. Immediately below this we were able to distinguish the clean-cut earth sides of a pit, sloping inwards and smoothly plastered with mud; following these down, we found the largest death-pit that the cemetery has yet produced. The pit was roughly rectangular and measured 37 feet by 24 at the bottom, and was approached as usual by a sloped ramp. In it lay the bodies of six men-servants and sixty-eight women; the men lay along the side by the door, the bodies of the women were disposed in regular rows across the floor, every one lying on her side with legs slightly bent and hands brought up near the face, so close together that the heads of those in one row rested on the legs of those in the row above. Here was to be observed even more clearly what had been fairly obvious in the graves of Shub-ad and her husband, the neatness with which the bodies were laid out, the entire absence of any signs of violence or terror.

We have often been asked how the victims in the royal graves met their death, and it is impossible to give a decisive answer. The bones are too crushed and too decayed to show any cause of death, supposing that violence had been used, but the general condition of the bodies does supply a strong argument. Very many of these women wear head-dresses which are delicate in themselves and would easily be disarranged, yet such are always found in good order, undisturbed except by the pressure of the earth; this would be impossible if the wearers had been knocked on the head, im-probable if they had fallen to the ground after being stabbed, and it is equally unlikely that they could have been killed outside the grave and carried down the ramp and laid in their places with all their ornaments intact; certainly the animals must have been alive when they dragged the chariots down the ramps, and if so, the grooms who led them and the drivers in the cars must have been alive also: it is safe to assume that those who were to be sacrificed went down alive into the pit.

That they were dead, or at least unconscious, when the earth was flung in and trampled down on the top of them is an equally safe assumption, for in any other case there must have been some struggle which would have left its traces in the attitude of the bodies, but these are always decently composed; indeed, they are in such good order and alignment that we are driven to suppose that after they were lying unconscious someone entered the pit and gave the final touches to their arrangement—and the circumstance that in A-bar-gi's grave the harps were placed on the top of the bodies proves that someone did enter the grave at the end. It is most probable that the victims walked to their places, took some kind of drug—opium or hashish would serve—and lay down in order; after the drug had worked, whether it produced sleep or death, the last touches were given to their bodies and the pit was filled in. There does not seem to have been anything brutal in the manner of their deaths.

None the less, the sight of the remains of the victims is gruesome enough with the gold leaves and the coloured beads lying thick on the crushed and broken skulls, but in excavating a great death-pit such as that of last winter we do not see it as a whole, but have to clear it a little at a time. The soil was removed until the bodies were almost exposed, covered only by the few inches of broken brick which had been the first of the filling thrown over the dead; here and there a pick driven too deep might bring to view a piece of gold ribbon or a golden beech leaf, showing that everywhere there were bodies richly adorned, but these would be quickly covered up again and left until more methodical work should reveal them in due course. Starting in one corner of the pit, we marked out squares such as might contain from five to six bodies, and all these were cleared, noted, and the objects belonging to them collected and removed before the next square was taken in hand.

It was slow work, and especially so in those cases where we decided to remove the entire skull with all its ornaments in position on it. The wreaths and chains and necklaces re-strung and arranged in a glass case may look very well, but it is more interesting to see them as they were actually found, and therefore a few heads on which the original order of the beads and gold-work was best preserved were laboriously cleaned with small knives and brushes, the dirt being removed without disturbing any of the ornaments—a difficult matter as they are loose in the soil—and then boiling paraffin wax was poured over them, solidifying them in one mass. The lump of wax, earth, bone, and gold was then strengthened by waxed cloth pressed carefully over it, so that it could be lifted from the ground by undercutting. Mounted in plaster, with the superfluous wax cleaned off, these heads form an exhibit which is not only of interest in itself but proves the accuracy of the restorations which we have made of others (Plate IV*a*).

Of the sixty-eight women in the pit, twenty-eight wore hair-ribbons of gold. At first sight it looked as if the others had nothing of the kind, but closer examination showed that many, if not all, had originally worn exactly similar ribbons of silver. Unfortunately silver is a metal which ill resists the action of the acids in the soil, and where it was but a thin strip and, being worn on the head, was directly affected by the corruption of the flesh, it generally disappears altogether, and at most there may be detected on the bone of the skull slight traces of a purplish colour which is silver chloride in a minutely powdered state: we could be certain that the ribbons were worn, but we could not produce material evidence of them.

But in one case we had better luck. The great gold

ear-rings were in place, but not a sign of discoloration
betrayed the existence of any silver head-dress, and
this negative evidence was duly noted: then, as the body
was cleared, there was found against it, about on the
level of the waist, a flat disk a little more than 3 inches
across of a grey substance which was certainly silver;
it might have been a small circular box. Only when I
was cleaning it in the house that evening, hoping to
find something which would enable me to catalogue
it more in detail, did its real nature come to light: it
was the silver hair-ribbon, but it had never been worn
—carried apparently in the woman's pocket, it was
just as she had taken it from her room, done up in a
tight coil with the ends brought over to prevent its coming
undone; and since it formed thus a comparatively
solid mass of metal and had been protected by the cloth
of her dress, it was very well preserved and even the
delicate edges of the ribbon were sharply distinct.
Why the owner had not put it on one could not say;
perhaps she was late for the ceremony and had not
time to dress properly, but her haste has in any case
afforded us the only example of a silver hair-ribbon
which we are likely ever to find.

Another thing that perishes utterly in the earth is
cloth, but occasionally on lifting a stone bowl which
has lain inverted over a bit of stuff and has protected
it from the soil one sees traces which, although only
of fine dust, keep the texture of the material, or a copper
vessel may by its corrosion preserve some fragment
which was in contact with it. By such evidence we were
able to prove that the women in the death-pit wore
garments of bright red woollen stuff; and as many of
them had at the wrists one or two cuffs made of beads
which had been sewn on to cloth, it was tolerably certain
that these were sleeved coats rather than cloaks. It
must have been a very gaily dressed crowd that assembled
in the open mat-lined pit for the royal obsequies, a blaze

of colour with the crimson coats, the silver, and the gold; clearly these people were not wretched slaves killed as oxen might be killed, but persons held in honour, wearing their robes of office, and coming, one hopes, voluntarily to a rite which would in their belief be but a passing from one world to another, from the service of a god on earth to that of the same god in another sphere.

This much I think we can safely assume. Human sacrifice was confined exclusively to the funerals of royal persons, and in the graves of commoners, however rich, there is no sign of anything of the sort, not even such substitutes, clay figurines, etc., as are so common in Egyptian tombs and appear there to be a reminiscence of an ancient and more bloody rite. In much later times Sumerian kings were deified in their lifetime and honoured as gods after their death: the prehistoric kings of Ur were in their obsequies so distinguished from their subjects because they too were looked upon as superhuman, earthly deities; and when the chroniclers wrote in the annals of Sumer that 'after the Flood kingship again descended from the gods,' they meant no less than this. If the king, then, was a god, he did not die as men die, but was translated; and it might there-fore be not a hardship but a privilege for those of his court to accompany their master and continue in his service.

In the furnishing of the royal graves one constant feature is the harp or lyre; in this great death-pit there were no less than four lyres. One of these was the most magnificent that we have yet found; its sounding-box was bordered with a broad edging of mosaic in red and white and blue, the two uprights were encrusted with shell and lapis lazuli and red stone arranged in zones separated by wide gold bands, the cross-bar was half of plain wood, half plated with silver, shell plaques engraved with animal scenes adorned the front, and above these projected a splendid head of a bearded bull wrought in heavy gold (Plate V*a*). A second lyre was all of silver with a silver cow's head in front of the sounding-box, which was decorated with a narrow blue and white border and with shell plaques; a third, also of silver, was in the form of a high-prowed boat on which stood a statue of a stag sculptured in the round; the fourth, of wood but with two copper statues of stags, was almost entirely decayed, so much so that we cannot even be certain that it was a harp at all, but the first three instruments were in good condition and are amongst the finest objects found in the cemetery.

The commonest decoration of a harp or lyre is the head of an animal, and we now have the bearded bull, the cow, and, in an instrument of different form, the stag, though in this case the complete beast is shown; the difference is not, however, so great as might appear, because in the other cases the sounding-box itself represents, though in a highly conventional, not to say 'cubist' form, the body of the animal, resolved almost entirely into straight lines, but still recognisable as such.

Now, there is an inscription by a governor Gudea (it is true that he lived a thousand years later, but tradition also is long-lived) in which he describes a harp he had presented to a temple; it was decorated with the head of a bull, and the sound of the instrument is compared to the bellowing of the beast. If there exists such a connection between the tone of the harp and the figure represented on it, might we not assume that our instruments are of three different sorts, the bull denoting the bass, the cow the tenor, and the stag perhaps the alto ? Then the finding of four lyres together in one grave might imply a system of harmony which, at this early date, would be of very great interest for the history of music.

In a corner of the same pit there were lying two statues made of gold, lapis lazuli, and white shell; slightly different in size, they were otherwise a pair, the subject being the same in each case. On a small oblong base decorated with silver plate and mosaic in pink and white stands a goat 'a ram of the goats,' erect on its hind legs in front of a tree or bush to whose branches its front legs were bound with silver chains; the leaves and flowers of the golden tree stand out high on either side, and the beast's golden head with its horns and hair of lapis lazuli peers out between them (Plate VI). Irresistibly we are reminded of the biblical story of the 'ram caught in the thicket,' but the statues were made fifteen hundred years before Abraham was born and the parallel is therefore difficult to explain. Undoubtedly the subject of the Sumerian sculpture had some religious significance; this and similar scenes are common in the artistic repertoire of the early period and probably illustrate some well-known legend, and there is no reason to suppose that legend and illustration did not survive into a later time: the writer in Genesis may well have taken advantage of a familiar reference to point the moral of his own story; in any case, we have here a striking anticipation of his phrase.

When the earth was thrown back into the death-pit and the tomb-chamber of the king and the bodies of the victims around it had been buried out of sight, the ritual of burial was far from being complete. Generally the upper soil of the cemetery has been so disturbed by later interments and by tomb-robbers that for a long time we failed to find any evidence of the subsequent stages of the ceremony, but in the season 1928–9 we were more fortunate.

We had been digging a patch of ground where, near the surface, the graves of commoners lay unusually thick, and were surprised to find that the shaft of one of them, containing a clay coffin, had been cut into a stout mud-brick wall. Working against the face of this, we came upon a number of clay jars, an alabaster vase, and a rectangle of faint grey lines which represented a wooden box. Scraping away the surface soil, we discovered in the box, lying side by side, two daggers of which the blades were of gold and the hilts decorated with gold studs, and between them a white shell cylinder seal inscribed with the name 'Mes-kalam-dug the King.' Next to the box was a wooden coffin containing the body of a man, but the furniture with it was by no means of the type which one would expect with a royal person, and the wall not only went further down into the soil, but as we followed it out developed into a large square of which the coffin occupied only a humble corner; we felt sure that we had not yet found the king's grave.

Under the floor of beaten clay on which the coffin rested more clay vessels appeared forming a consistent layer over the whole area of the brick enclosure, and with these, but in another corner than that occupied by the coffin, was a second burial of a man with his weapons and vases of copper and stone. This clay floor was removed, and a fresh layer of pots and another burial came to light, and below this more layers of offerings alternating with layers of clay. Then came clean filling extending to the base of the brick walls, and at this level a single great clay bowl put upside-down in the earth sheltering two or three little food-bowls set out on a piece of matting—the meal spread for the god of the underworld.

We dug deeper down, and suddenly limestone blocks appeared bedded in green clay and forming a curve; we took it to be the end of a stone vault, and when the stones quickly dipped again feared that the roof had been broken through by robbers; but another half-hour's work proved to our delight that the masonry continued and that what we had was a small dome absolutely intact. It was particularly exciting because the top of the dome had been built over a centring supported by stout beams which ran right through the stone-work, and the decay of these had left half a dozen holes in the roof through which one could glimpse parts of the dim interior and by the light of electric torches could even see on the floor below the shapes of green copper vessels and catch an occasional glint of gold.

We cleared down to the level of the tops of the walls of the tomb-chamber, and at each corner, resting on the heavy clay which filled the space between the walls and the sides of the pit, found the ashes of fires and broken clay pots and animal bones. In front of the chamber door were laid the carcases of three sheep. The stone blocking of the door was pulled away, and inside, beneath the remains of rotten wood fallen from the ceiling lay five bodies; four of them were those of men—servants, judging from their poor equipment, and the fifth was that of a woman; she had the golden head-dress of one of high rank, a long curved golden pin such as we had not seen before fastened her cloak, in her hands was a fluted and engraved tumbler of gold, and by her side a golden cylinder seal, the first we have ever found: this clearly was the queen.

Now the ritual of the interment could be understood. The royal body with its attendants, many or few, was laid in the tomb, and the door was sealed and sacrifice was made in the little court before the entrance, and then this was filled in until only the crown of the dome was left above ground. Round it fires were lit and a funeral feast was held, and libations to the dead were poured into a clay drain which ran down into the soil beside the tomb, and then more earth was thrown into the shaft. Next an offering to the under-gods was set out and covered with a clay bowl to shield it from the fresh earth which buried it; and then, in the half-filled pit, there was constructed in mud brick what was to be a subterranean building.

The filling-up of this building was done by degrees; clay was brought and trampled hard to make a floor over which offerings were spread and on which was laid the body of a human victim sacrificed in these later rites; earth buried these, and another floor was made and more offerings placed in order and another victim did honour to the dead below, and this went on till the top of the walls was nearly reached; then half of the building was roofed in with a vault of mud brick, and in this subsidiary tomb was put the coffin of one whom we may suppose to have been the chief sacrifice, and here King Mes-kalam-dug dedicated to the un-named queen his golden daggers and the seal bearing his title. Then this chamber too was buried under the filling of the shaft, and probably on the top of it all there was erected on the ground-surface some kind of funerary chapel which should perpetuate the sanctity of the spot.

Each stage of this elaborate procedure must have been marked by some religious service, and the whole ceremony must have taken a long time; the details of it very likely varied in different cases, but the discovery of a second royal tomb (unfortunately plundered) with layers of offerings above it exactly corresponding to that just described proves that this is no isolated case but illustrates the normal ritual for the burial of a king.

As I have said above, there was no such ritual for the commoner. Last winter we found the grave of a 'court lady' wearing the golden head-dress familiar to us from the royal tombs, and amongst the offerings set alongside her coffin there was even a harp, a simpler edition of the type found with Queen Shub-ad; but here there were no victims sacrificed in her honour, and we can only suppose that she was a private person and that the harp was her personal property which she wished to take with her to another world, just as someone else might take a gaming-board or a toilet-box.

The body of a little girl not more than six or seven years old was adorned with a head-dress almost as elaborate as Queen Shub-ad's own, but on a miniature scale, tiny gold rings across the forehead, tiny gold beech leaves hanging from the strings of lapis and carnelian beads; she grasped a gold cup only about 2 inches high, and by her side were two silver bowls and a fluted tumbler reproducing in miniature those from the queen's tomb; our workmen called this 'the grave of the little princess,' but she lay in it alone and could boast none of the blood-offerings of kings. But the best proof of the gulf that separated king from commoner was given by the grave of Mes-kalam-dug discovered in the season 1927–8, a grave dug down into the shaft of the largest of all the stone-built royal tombs.

The first indication we had of what was to come was a copper spear-head sticking straight up in the ground; following this down we found that it was attached to a golden haft, and below this was the hole left by the decay of the wooden shaft running down to a corner of the grave. Except for the fact that it was rather larger than usual, the grave was a normal one, a plain earth pit big enough to take a wooden coffin and to leave on three sides of this a free space for offerings. Along the head of the grave were stuck spears in a row, the blades downwards, and between these were vases of alabaster and clay; by the side of the coffin, lying on the remains of what may have been a bossed shield, were two gold-mounted daggers, copper daggers, chisels and other tools, some fifty copper bowls, many of them fluted, and other bowls of silver, copper jugs and plates, and more vessels of stone and clay; at the foot of the grave again spears, and with them a set of arrows having chisel-edged points of chipped flint.

But it was when the earth from the coffin itself was removed that we had our great surprise—and as the discovery was made soon after our disappointment with the first of the stone-built royal graves, when only the golden dagger of the year before had given us an inkling of what treasures the cemetery might yield, our surprise was the greater. The body lay in normal fashion on its right side; round the waist was a broad belt of silver, now decayed, from which hung a gold dagger and a whetstone of lapis lazuli fixed on a gold ring; in front of the waist was a solid mass of lapis and gold beads, hundreds in all; between the hands was placed a bowl of heavy gold, a larger oval gold bowl lay close by, and near the elbow a gold lamp in the form of a shell, while yet another gold bowl stood behind the head. Against the right shoulder was a double axe-head of electrum, and an electrum axe-head of normal type was by the left shoulder; behind the body there were jumbled together in a heap a gold head-dress, bracelets, beads, and amulets, lunate earrings, and spiral rings of gold wire.

The bones were so far decayed that there was here none of the grimness of a skeleton, only a few strips of crumbling brown which served to show the attitude of the dead man, and the prevailing note was struck rather by the gold, clean as when it was put into the grave; and most of all was the eye taken by the helmet which still covered the rotten fragments of the skull. It was a helmet of beaten gold made to fit low over the head with cheek-pieces to protect the face, and it was in the form of a wig, the locks of hair hammered up in relief, the individual hairs shown by delicate engraved lines. Parted down the middle the hair covers the head in flat wavy tresses and is bound round with a twisted fillet; behind it is tied into a little chignon, and below the fillet hangs in rows of formal curls about the ears, which are rendered in high relief and are pierced so as not to interfere with hearing; similar curls on the cheek-pieces represent whiskers; round the edge of the metal are small holes for the laces which secured inside it a padded cap, of which some traces yet remained.

As an example of goldsmith's work this is the most beautiful thing we have found in the cemetery, finer than the gold daggers or the heads of bulls, and if there were nothing else by which the art of these ancient Sumerians could be judged we should still, on the strength of it alone, accord them high rank in the roll of civilised races.

On two of the golden bowls and on the lamp was repeated the inscription 'Mes-kalam-dug, Hero of the Good Land.' The name is the same as that found on the cylinder seal dedicated with the two gold daggers above the domed stone tomb of a queen but the owner of the deal is called 'King,' and here there is no such title of royalty: the term 'Hero of the Good Land' and the exceptional richness of the grave may justify us in seeing in this Mes-kalam-dug a prince of the royal house, but the omission of any claim to kingly power ought certainly to mean that he never occupied the throne, and this omission is precisely what we should expect if our theory is correct, for the grave is essentially of the commoner's type and contains no subsidiary burials, no hint of human sacrifice. Had the royal tombs not been discovered, this would probably have been hailed as a king's grave; as it is, its wealth only emphasises the difference between it and them.

While trying to give some idea of what the graves are like and describing some of the treasures they contain, I have said very little about the condition of the objects at the time of finding. It is true that no imagination was required to grasp the splendour of Mes-kalam-dug's grave, because the objects in that were for the most part of gold, and gold is imperishable; a gold bowl may be crushed or dinted, but its colour and its surface remain and every detail of its workmanship and decoration is as clear as when it was newly wrought; but other materials are less enduring—I have spoken of the way in which silver corrodes and even vanishes—and suffer both from internal decay and from the crushing weight of the 30 or 40 feet of earth below which they have lain buried for five thousand years. Often it is difficult to remove from the soil without further damage an object which it is essential to preserve; sometimes it is hard even to judge of the object's nature and importance; nearly always some measure of repair or restoration is required before the thing is fit for exhibition, and the restoration may be the most laborious task of all.

As an illustration of this I would take one of the two statues of rams found in the great death-pit. The figure was made as follows. The head and legs were carved in wood, the horns of lapis and the inlaid eyes being fixed in position by copper rivets driven through the head, and then gold, little thicker than gold leaf, was laid over them, a thin wash of bitumen acting as glue to fix the metal on to the wood. The head and legs were mortised into a rudimentary wooden body which was next rounded off into proper shape with plaster of paris and given a thick coat of bitumen; a thin silver plate was fixed over the belly, and into the bitumen covering back and sides were pressed the locks of hair, each carved separately from a piece of white shell, or, for the shoulders, in lapis lazuli; the tree was also of wood overlaid with gold leaf, the leaves and flowers made of double gold and fixed on after the trunk and branches were complete.

When we found them, both statues were in very sorry plight. The wood had decayed to nothing, the bitumen was dry powder, the plaster of paris reduced to irregular lumps and pellets; one figure was lying on its side, crushed absolutely flat so that the shell curls of the two flanks touched each other and the animal was a mere silhouette distorted by pressure, the other, standing upright, preserved some of its roundness but had been telescoped together and the legs had been broken off from the body, flattened and twisted. Nothing except the earth around them kept the fragments of lapis and shell inlay in position, and if that position were once lost, there would have been no guide at all for the restoration of the figure; the whole thing was therefore solidified with hot wax poured liberally on, and then bands of waxed muslin were applied to every exposed part until the ram was as securely wrapped up as a mummy and could be lifted from the earth.

For restoration, the waxed wrappings were softened with heat sufficiently for the sides of the beast to be pressed apart and the dirt removed from inside its body; then wax and bandages were applied to the interior, the outer bandages removed, and with gentle heating the body could be pushed out into its original shape, and that without dislodging the inlaid locks of the fleece now adhering to the inner coating of wax. The complete decay of the silver over the belly really facilitated the task, because it gave a chance to work at the body from the inside through a comparatively large opening. The legs were straightened, and with slender tools inserted down the tubes of them the dinted gold was pressed out again as much as possible, then copper wires were put down them and a boiling mixture of wax and bitumen poured in to make all solid. The head presented greater difficulties, because the thin gold lead was broken into eighteen small fragments and these were badly crushed and bent; each had to be unfolded, worked out to its original curve and strengthened from the back, and then the joints had to be found and the different morsels brought together and fixed with due regard to the curves of their outer face. It was a jigsaw puzzle in three dimensions, but in time the head took shape and character. Plastic wood was used to fill the body and to secure the wires of the legs, the belly was painted with silver paint to replace the perished metal, and the statue was complete (Plate VI).

Of course, methods of this kind cannot reproduce all the *finesse* of the original; to do that one would have to take the whole thing to pieces and re-create; but in so doing one loses something which is of sentimental if not always of scientific importance—the object as exhibited is really a copy, new throughout, of the old work, and no one can be quite certain of its faithfulness. In dealing with the antiquities from Ur we have preferred a restoration which implies the least possible interference with the object to a reconstruction which may give a better appearance but depends more on the modern hand.

Another instance will make the point clearer. In the largest of all the stone-built royal tombs, which had been entered by robbers and most thoroughly plundered, there remained only one corner of the last chamber to be cleared, and we had given up expectation of any 'finds' when suddenly a loose bit of shell inlay turned up, and the next minute the foreman's hand, carefully brushing away the earth, laid bare the corner of a mosaic in lapis lazuli and shell. This was the famous 'Standard' of Ur, but at the time we had very little idea of what it might be: the wooden background had perished entirely, and the tiny pieces of inlay, though they kept their relative positions in the soil, were all quite loose; falling stones had bent and twisted the once flat panel, while as the wood decayed and the fragments sank back into the empty space behind, their different thickness made the surface of them rough and uneven. So delicate was the task of removing the dirt without further disturbing the mosaic that only about a square inch could be dealt with at a time—each section was waxed as soon as cleared, but so much of the surrounding dirt mingled with the hot wax that the face of the panel became invisible.

When at last it could be lifted from the earth, I knew that we had found a very fine thing, but should have been hard put to it to say exactly what it was.

Now, it would have been perfectly feasible to take the mosaic to pieces, bit by bit, and re-make it on a new background, and the task might have been done as well by the modern craftsman as by the old, but the panels would have been the work of a modern craftsman.

What was done was this. The two sides of the panel were separated, and waxed cloth was fixed to the back of the inlay and the face of it was roughly cleaned; it was then laid face downwards on glass and warmed until the wax was soft, and it was pressed with the fingers from behind until by looking underneath one could be sure that each fragment of the inlay was in direct contact with the glass. The panel was now flat, but the pattern was much distorted; the edges of the mosaic fragments had lost contact in the ground and earth and powdered bitumen had filtered between them, and now wax as well, so that while some overlapped, others were widely apart. The next stage was to remove the cloth from the back, leaving the mosaic virtually loose on the glass, and to pick out all foreign matter, and then by sideways pressure with the fingers coax the pieces together. When this was done, fresh wax and cloth were applied behind and a proper backing fixed on.

The result of this is that the mosaic is not nearly so regular or smooth as the Sumerian artist made it, but what we possess is the work of that artist uninterfered with except by the accidents of time; the pieces of shell and lapis which he put together no one else has taken apart and re-set (Plate VII).

In the case of the 'Standard' the labour of restoration was at the same time a process of discovery; the work in the field had really been done in the dark, and it was only when the panels were cleaned and had begun to take shape in the laboratory that their importance could be recognised. There are two main panels, rectangular and measuring 22 inches long by 9 inches high, and two triangular pieces which formed the ends; these were fixed together so that the larger sides sloped inwards and the whole thing was fastened on to the end of a pole, and would seem to have been carried in processions; we actually found it lying against the shoulder of a man who may have been the king's standard-bearer.

The mosaic is composed of figures silhouetted in shell with details engraved which are set in a background of lapis lazuli, relieved here and there with red. The triangular ends have mythological scenes of animals; the main panels illustrate respectively Peace and War. On one side the king and the royal family are seen at feast. They sit in chairs, their costume consists of the old-fashioned sheep-skin kilt or petticoat and the upper part of the body is bare; servants wait on them, and at one end of the scene is a musician playing on a small harp, while by him a woman singer with her hands to her breast sings to the accompaniment of the instrument.

These figures form the top row of the design; in two lower rows attendants are shown bringing in spoils captured from the enemy and food-supplies for the banquet—one is driving a goat, another carries two fish, another is bent under the weight of a corded bale, and so on, several of the figures being repeated. On the other side, in the centre of the top row, stands the king, distinguished by his greater height, with behind him three attendants or members of his house, and a dwarf-like groom who holds the heads of the two asses which draw the monarch's empty chariot while the driver of it walks behind holding the reins; in front of the king soldiers are bringing up prisoners, naked and with their arms bound behind their backs, for him to decide their fate.

In the second row, at the back, comes the phalanx of the royal army, heavy-armed infantry in close order with copper helmets exactly like those found by us in the king's grave, and long cloaks of some stiff material which I take to be felt, just such cloaks as are worn by the shepherds of Anatolia to-day, holding axes in their hands; in front of them are the light-armed infantry without cloaks, wielding axes or short spears, already engaged with an enemy whose naked warriors are either fleeing or being struck down.

In the lowest row we have the chariotry of Sumer, each car drawn by two asses and carrying two men, of whom one is the driver and the other a warrior who flings light javelins, of which four are kept in a quiver tied to the front of the car. The chariots advance over the battlefield, and by a naturalistic touch the artist of the 'Standard' makes the asses at the rear walk sedately, while those drawing the other cars become more and more excited as they encounter the corpses strewn on the ground, until those in front have broken into a gallop which threatens the balance of the riders.

The 'Standard' is a remarkable work of art, but it has yet greater value as an historical document, for here we have figured the earliest detailed picture of that army which carried the civilisation of the Sumerians from their early settlements on the fringe of the Persian Gulf to the mountains of Anatolia and to the shores of the Mediterranean Sea. We know from actual examples found in their graves that their weapons were, both in design and in manufacture, far superior to anything that their contemporaries possessed or any other nation was to adopt for two thousand years; from this representation we can learn enough about the organisation of the army to know that it must have been more than a match for anything that could be brought against it at that time. The chariotry which

was to inspire an almost superstitious terror in the
Hebrews of the time of the Judges had been used by
the Sumerians more than two thousand years before,
and the phalanx which won Alexander his victories
had been anticipated by them: it is not surprising that
until they had taught their neighbours to profit by their
example they found no opponent to withstand their
advance.

This is the story of the excavations at Ur, not a
history of the Sumerian people, but something must
be said here to show how important those excavations
have been for our knowledge of early civilisation. The
contents of the tombs illustrate a very highly developed
state of society of an urban type, a society in which the
architect was familiar with all the basic principles of
construction known to us to-day. The artist, capable
at times of a most vivid realism, followed for the most
part standards and conventions whose excellence had
been approved by many generations working before
him; the craftsman in metal possessed a knowledge of
metallurgy and a technical skill which few ancient
peoples ever rivalled; the merchant carried on a far-
flung trade and recorded his transactions in writing;
the army was well organised and victorious, agriculture
prospered, and great wealth gave scope to luxury.
Our tombs date, as has already been said, between
3500 and 3200 B.C., and as the nature of the civilisation
would lead one to expect, and as has been demon-
strated by the discoveries in the rubbish below the
tombs described in the last chapter, by 3500 B.C. this
civilisation was already many centuries old.

Until recently it was thought that the Egyptian
civilisation was the oldest in the world and that it
was the fountain-head wherefrom the later civilisations
of other Western countries drew at any rate the inspira-
tion which informed them. But in 3500 B.C. Egypt
was still barbarous, divided into petty kingdoms not

yet united by 'Menes,' the founder of the First Dynasty, into a single state. When Egypt does make a start, the beginnings of a new age are marked by the introduction of models and ideas which derive from that older civilisation which, as we know now, had long been developing and flourishing in the Euphrates valley, and to the Sumerians we can trace much that is at the root not only of Egyptian, but also of Babylonian, Assyrian, Hebrew, and Phœnician art and thought, and so see that the Greeks also were in debt to this ancient and for long forgotten people, the pioneers of the progress of Western man. It is this that makes excavation in the oldest levels at Ur of such absorbing interest, the knowledge that almost every object found is not merely an illustration of the achievement of a particular race at a particular time, but also a new document helping to fill up the picture of those beginnings from which is derived our modern world.

PLATE I

(*a*) Painted pottery of the period before the Flood.

(*b*) Flint implements and clay models of tools from before the Flood.

PLATE II

Ground plan of the royal tomb (Pg/789). The grave of King
A-bar-gi. The bodies of the human victims, waggons, etc., are
shown in position. The chamber above (Pg/800) is that of Queen
Shub-ad.

PLATE III

(*a*) Silver model of a boat from Tomb Pg/789.

(*b*)

(*c*)

(*b* and *c*) Gold vessels of Queen Shub-ad.

PLATE IV

(a)   (b)

(a) Woman's head-dress from the Great Death-pit.
(b) The gold dagger at Ur.

PLATE **V**

(*a*) Gold and mosaic harp from the Great Death-pit.

(*b*) An inlaid gaming-board.

PLATE VI

The statue of 'a ram caught in a thicket.'

PLATE VII

The mosaic 'Standard' of Ur.

PLATE VIII

(*a*) Mosaic frieze from the temple at al 'Ubaid.

(*b*) The temple at al 'Ubaid restored.

PLATE IX

(a) The south-west face of Ur-Nammu's Ziggurat.

(b) The Ziggurat restored.

PLATE X

(*a*) The angel pours out water on the earth.

(*b*) The King receives the order to build the Ziggurat.

The Stela of Ur-Nammu.

PLATE XI

(a) The memorial stones of Bur-Sin in the Moon-goddess's temple.

(b) The court-yard of the Moon-goddess's temple (in the centre, the brick base for Hammurabi's war memorial).

PLATE XII

Restoration of a house of the time of Abraham.

PLATE XIII

(*a*) The house of the time of Abraham: photograph taken from the same point of view as the restored drawing.

(*b*) A domestic chapel, showing the altar and niche and the family vault below the broken floor of the nave.

PLATE XIV

(*a*) Clay figures from under the floor of a late building.

(*b*) The shrine Dublal-makh, showing Kuri-Galzu's platform.

PLATE XV

(*a*) The face of the great Temenos Wall of Nebuchadnezzar.

(*b*) The temple of E-Nun-makh. The part of the building as remodelled by Nebuchadnezzar, showing the altar in part of the sanctuary door, the pavement of the upper court and, in the corner, one of Kuri-galzu's chambers underlying the broken floor of the lower court.

PLATE XVI

(a) A Kassite boundary-stone from Bel-Shalti-Nannar's museum.

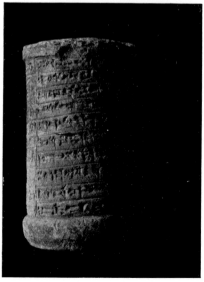

(b) The clay 'label' from Bel-Shalti-Nannar's museum.

CHAPTER III

AL 'UBAID AND THE EARLIEST WRITTEN HISTORY

In 1919 Dr. H. R. Hall, working for the British Museum, found, in what might be called a suburb of Ur, a little mound some four miles from the centre of the city, ruins of very early date and very remarkable character. He traced round three sides the outer face of a rectangular building constructed with the small round-topped bricks called 'plano-convex' which are only used in the earliest times, and against one face came upon a hoard of objects lying tumbled together under a mass of mud brick.

There was a small stone statue of a man carved in the primitive and summary style already familiar to us from stray examples procured elsewhere, but with this were other monuments of a more novel sort. There was a great copper relief 7 ft. 9 ins. long and 3 ft. 6 ins. high, representing in heraldic fashion an eagle grasping two stags; there were the fore parts of lions, nearly life-size, made of copper hammered over bitumen and wood with inlaid eyes and white shell teeth through which protruded tongues of red stone; there were fragments of wooden columns incrusted with mother-of-pearl, red stone, and black shale; clay flowers with inlaid petals of white, black, and red, and more heads of animals in copper but on a smaller scale. Altogether it was a most important discovery, and since the excavation was left unfinished by Dr. Hall, it was the obvious duty of the Joint Expedition to complete it as soon as possible. In the season 1923–4, therefore, a branch camp was set up at al 'Ubaid (such is the name of the

little mound), and the work was re-started with the
hope that more light would be thrown on the nature
of the building and that there might yet be objects
awaiting discovery.

Dr. Hall's work had given us a warning. The copper
statues found by him had suffered terribly through
corrosion and breakage, and, important as they were,
were but ghosts of the originals; of the lions' heads
little more remained than the bitumen cores with the
inlay of eyes and mouth, of the columns only the loose
fragments of the incrustation, could be collected and
brought home, and the great copper relief, of which
only one stag's head was recovered intact, had to be
reconstructed from fragments, and in several respects
the reconstruction was open to doubt. If, then, we
should encounter any further objects of the kind we
had to be sure that our resources would be adequate
to the delicate task of their removal and transport.

The work of excavation which had produced the
original hoard of statuary had begun at one corner of
the building and had been carried on not quite to its
central point when the diggers had encountered and
partly cut into a particularly solid mass of mud brick.
We started at this point and, following up the brickwork—with some difficulty, for it showed no true face
—found that it was one side of a staircase projecting
at right angles from the main building; the treads,
of which a number were preserved at the stairs'
foot, were great slabs of white limestone, the first
example of the use of stone for building that had been
noted in the south of Mesopotamia except for a similar
flight of stairs leading up to the staged tower of Abu
Shahrein, a ruin about 12 miles south of Ur. Further
examination proved that the building itself was a solid
mass of brick, a platform approached by the flight
of steps, and only the substructure of a building which
itself had completely disappeared.

Working round the stairway and following the wall between it and the far corner of the platform we found, under a mass of mud brick of a later period (a new platform laid down over the ruins of the old), a second hoard of objects in part similar to those which had rewarded Dr. Hall and in part different. In the angle between the stairs and the wall there lay two ten-foot columns of wood encrusted with mother-of-pearl, shale, and red stone, and other palm-log columns and beams overlaid with sheets of copper; piled in one heap there were four copper statues of bulls standing upright with their heads turned outwards over their shoulders; in a line along the wall were copper reliefs of reclining cattle, and mixed with these sections of mosaic friezes in which figures silhouetted in white lime-stone or in shell were set against a background of black shale and framed with strips of copper; and everywhere in the soil we found fragments or complete examples of the inlaid clay flowers with cone-like stems which had figured in the earlier excavations.

One day a workman unearthed before my eyes a small oblong tablet of white limestone bearing an inscription; I handed it to Mr. Gadd, who was standing beside me, and he read it out: 'A-anni-pad-da King of Ur, son of Mes-anni-pad-da King of Ur, has built this for his Lady Nin-kharsag.' It was the foundation-stone of the building, and the most important of all our discoveries.

At first reading it does not sound a very exciting thing, a list of rather unpronounceable names, but we were excited enough. The first name was unknown to us or anyone, but the second was familiar, and not only proved the date of the building but cleared up a whole chapter in ancient history.

There exist copies, dating back before 2000 B.C., of lists drawn up by Sumerian scribes of the kings who, according to their successive dynasties, ruled the lower

valley of the Two Rivers. The later dynasties were
known to be historical, because independent monuments
of their kings had been found, but the earlier dynasties
had been rejected by modern students as mythical,
partly because nothing was known about them, mainly
because the scribes who composed the lists attributed
to the early rulers a longevity which outdoes Methuselah.
The third dynasty after the Flood is in the lists assigned
to the kings of Ur and is called the First Dynasty of
Ur, and its founder, who is given a reign of eighty
years, is Mes-anni-pad-da and is succeeded by Meskiag-
Nannar.

Now we had in our hands a contemporary written
document which proved the existence of the founder
of the First Dynasty of Ur and established the historical
truth of the ancient king-lists, while at the same time
it cleared up the only difficulty which they presented.
Mes-anni-pad-da had a son who does not appear in
the lists, but who actually succeeded his father on the
throne, and the names of the two were so much alike
that a not unnatural confusion resulted, and the reigns
of the two were lumped together and their total
span of eighty years attributed to the better-known
founder of the royal house; divide that figure by inserting
A-anni-pad-da's reign, and the only improbability
disappears. But our tablet not only proved the accuracy
of the written lists; it gave to our building a more or
less accurate date, about 3100 B.C., so that the objects
belonging to it could be considered in their proper
place in the sequence of the development of art; and
it meant that the First Dynasty of Ur was no longer
just a list of names, but stood for a period in history
whose character and achievements we now have material
to judge; a whole age was resuscitated and made real
by that one small stone.

But the objects to which so much extra interest was
lent by the finding of the foundation-tablet gave us a

very anxious time; they lay so thickly in the ground that there might be half a dozen of them all exposed at one time and all calling for special care in their removal; and their condition was quite as bad as we had feared.

The uppermost of the four copper bulls was barely recognisable, only part of one leg and a mass of green powder betraying its existence. The second looked more promising, but the metal was broken into a thousand pieces and was so soft that it crumbled to dust at a touch (I spent three weeks preparing it and then when we lifted it the whole thing collapsed in atoms); with the next two we had better success and they are now in the British Museum and at Philadelphia, battered and distorted figures but still figures of bulls showing something of the fine quality of the originals and remarkable as being the oldest copper statues preserved to us. The copper reliefs were less difficult to manage and only one was rejected as too fragmentary for removal, and even then the head, cast in metal and more solid than the hammered sheets which formed the body, remained a first-class object.

The inlaid columns were crushed flat and the wood had perished, but most of the tesseræ were approximately in position, only those along the edges having been dislodged and scattered. They were removed in sections, sacking being waxed on to the tesseræ that lay face upwards and glued on to the backs of those which belonged to the lower face of the shafts: lifted thus in sheets, the decoration could be fixed on to a new core (it was found that circular petrol-drums were of exactly the right diameter, and these served our turn) without any disturbance of the individual bits of stone and mother-of-pearl, while other sheets and the loose tesseræ collected from the earth were kept with a view to more drastic reconstruction.

The mosaic friezes were held together with wax and

muslin for such treatment as the Museum authorities might choose to give them. The friezes were two in number. One was simple, a row of birds, probably doves, rather roughly cut in white limestone (which I think was originally painted in colour) against a black ground. The other was much more elaborate and showed much finer workmanship. It consisted for most of its length of a procession of cows carved in limestone, probably once painted, or in shell, which was probably left white, but in the centre there was a scene in which human figures are introduced; on one side of a reed-built byre, from the door of which two calves are seen issuing, men seated on low stools are milking cattle; the man sits under the cow's tail milking her from behind; the calves, duly muzzled, are roped to the cows' head-stalls so as to encourage them to give milk. On the other side of the byre two men, shaven and wearing the fleece petticoat which in later times seems to survive as the official dress of priests and priest-kings, are pouring milk through a strainer into a vessel set on the ground, while two others are collecting the strained liquid in great store-jars (Plate VIII *a*).

It is a typical scene of pastoral life, but the costume of the actors makes it likely that it is something more than this. There were in later days at least sacred farms attached to the temples, and here we may have priests preparing the milk of the Mother-goddess Nin-kharsag which was the nourishment of kings. That the very domestic-looking picture of milking had a religious bearing is made more likely by the fact that in the same frieze there was introduced between the figures of walking cattle a small panel of a curiously incongruous character: it shows a bearded bull rampant in hilly country, on whose back is perched a lion-headed eagle apparently attacking him and tearing at his rump; this is certainly an illustration of some mythological legend

and its presence here cannot but affect our view of the
frieze as a whole.

All the objects found were clearly elements in the
architectural decoration of the building and would gain
enormously in interest if they could be assigned to their
proper place in the scheme. This was not easy, because
of the building itself there was not a single brick left
in position, and of the platform which supported it
the upper part had been destroyed, so that even the
ground-plan was unknown. Fortunately, it proved
possible, by taking the exact position of every object
in its relation to the wall and the exact angle at which
it lay, and by calculating the slope of the layers of
debris against the wall-face and the height of the objects
in that debris, to get a very fairly accurate idea of the
position from which each had fallen or, where things
had been thrown out, of the place from which the
people who violently destroyed the temple must have
thrown them, and so to work out the original plan
and character of the building (Plate VIII b).

The temple proper occupied one corner of the platform and its main door stood at the top of the flight
of stone steps; it stood a little back from the platform's
edge, and in front of its doors there was a porch with
a pent-house roof whose beams and supporting columns
were of wood overlaid with polished copper. Mosaic
columns held up the lintel, and above this was set into
the wall the copper relief of the eagle and two stags
found by Dr. Hall, while the front parts of lions found
by him had their place in re-entrant angles flanking
the actual doorway, which they thus seemed to guard.

On the ledge along the top of the platform, against
the background of the temple wall, stood the copper
statues of bulls, and round them, probably, were set
the clay flowers standing upright so as to give the
effect of animals in a flowery meadow. Higher up on
the façade came the copper frieze of reclining cattle

worked in relief; above these the mosaic frieze with
the milking-scene; and higher up still the bird frieze
with its bolder and more roughly-carved figures. The
brick balustrades of the staircase were certainly panelled
with wood, for we found along the foot of them the
copper nails by which the wood was attached; the
platform was of burnt brick below, and this may well
have been left exposed; the upper part, of mud brick,
was probably whitewashed, as was the mud-brick wall
of the temple above.

We can picture the whole building as something very
gay and fanciful, the gold and colour of its decoration
vivid against the white walls, and we can admire the
skill with which the elements of the decoration are
graded according to their height from the ground—
statues in the round below, then figures in relief, then
flat figures seen as silhouettes against the black bands
of the friezes—and the knowledge of perspective which
prefers simpler and broader effects for the top row of
all. We shall admire the more if we recognise that it
is the oldest building in Mesopotamia and one of the
earliest in the world which we can re-create more or
less as it really was.

In a second and smaller mound which lay close to
the temple we found a number of graves. Compared
with those of the early cemetery at Ur they were very
poor, containing as they did few objects other than
pottery, but they were, in spite of that, most important.
It was natural to suppose that they should be contemporary with A-anni-pad-da's building, since the
neighbourhood of a temple is holy ground and is
therefore generally a favourite spot for burying the
dead; but besides this, some of the clay vessels of very
distinctive form found in the graves were actually
represented in the milking-scene on the mosaic frieze;
the graves could be confidently assigned to the First
Dynasty of Ur, and since they supplied us with a great

variety of pottery types used in that period, we had
an admirable starting-point for dating subsequent discoveries.

In all excavations, whether in building sites or in
graveyards, pottery forms the bulk of the objects found.
In every country the forms of clay vessels in common
use change from age to age as civilisation advances or
degenerates, new social conditions have to be met,
new inventions are introduced or simply fashions alter:
a few types may be fairly constant throughout a long
period, but on the whole pots change with the times,
and while the same is true of all other things, pots,
as being the most numerous and, since baked clay is
for all its fragility virtually indestructible, the best
preserved, are the most useful evidence for dating.
In a country like Egypt, where the domestic pottery
of every age has been carefully studied and recorded,
it is possible to fix the age of a ruin by merely walking
over the mounds and observing the sherds which strew
the surface; in Mesopotamia in 1923 very little was
known of the pottery of any period and that of the
early times was absolutely unknown. To secure more
than a hundred shapes of vases and to learn the kind
of ware employed in making them, with the certainty
that all belonged to a definite period in history, was
most valuable, and when we came to excavate the rich
tombs of Ur it was partly on the basis of the graves
of al 'Ubaid that we were able to assign to them their
true date.

The First Dynasty of Ur, which with the discoveries
just described emerged from the mists of legend into
the world of reality, is poorly represented by buildings
in the city of Ur itself, at least so far as our excavations
have gone as yet. A few broken walls of 'plano-convex'
brick, in one case built like the platform of al 'Ubaid
on foundations of limestone blocks, are all that have
survived the ravages of time and the constant demolition

and re-building of old sites by men, but a certain
number of objects have come to light which belong to
that age.

In the cemetery two or three graves have been found
which seem to be later than the rest and may overlap
into the time of the First Dynasty, and probably there
were more which have been plundered and destroyed;
this would account for a discovery made at no great
depth from the modern surface, the discovery of a
lapis lazuli cylinder seal, lying loose in the soil and
coming from some ruined grave, on which was inscribed
the name of the wife of king Mes-anni-pad-da, the
mother, as we may suppose, of him who built the temple
at al 'Ubaid; two generations of the royal house are
now represented by contemporary inscriptions. On
grounds of style we may assign to the same date a stone
fragment found close to a First Dynasty brick floor
buried in the rubbish on the south-west outskirts of
the cemetery; it is the lower half of a limestone slab
on which is carved in relief a scene of the funeral procession of a king; the empty chariot, covered with a
spotted leopard's skin, drawn by two beasts which look
like lions but ought by analogy to be asses (their heads
are broken away), is led along by attendants; there
was another scene above which is lost.

Under the foundations of a house attached to one
of the temples another discovery was made. The
ground here had been terraced for the building, and
tumbled together in the filling behind the terrace wall
was a group of objects of First Dynasty date. Two
of these were a pair, limestone figures of rams, only
the heads and foreparts carved in the round, the rest
left rough; they seem to be supports for a throne,
probably the seat of some statue of a god whose sacred
emblem was the ram. With them was a small relief
in alabaster carved on both sides; it was badly weathered
and only half of it was preserved, but it was curiously

interesting. It represented a high-prowed boat made
of reeds tied together and having an arched cabin or
canopy amidships—a boat not unlike the silver model
found in the tomb of the king A-bar-gi; on one side
a man was shown standing in the stern and a sow in
the cabin, on the other two fish took the place of the
man and a goose that of the sow. Probably the little
object was dedicated in a temple by one of the marsh
folk and pictures the sort of life he led, for fish, wild
geese, and wild boar are the staple products of the
marsh-land; it was a strong temptation to call it a
picture of Noah's Ark ! but though that passed as a
jest in camp, the other is the more likely explanation !

The First Dynasty, when Ur was the capital of all
the South Country, must have been a very rich and
prosperous time, and at any moment we may light
upon some important work of its kings hidden under
the mounds of the city; but even without that we
have, thanks to al 'Ubaid, a remarkable illustration
of their achievements. The dynasty came to a violent
end and the sovereignty of Sumer passed to other
hands and to another city, and the long period of
subjection which followed is unmarked by any monuments. The work which we have done round the Ziggurat has afforded proof that already in the First
Dynasty there was a great staged tower attached to
the temple of the Moon-god, which is indeed no more
than we should expect, and some remains of mud-brick
walls there give evidence of repairs or rebuilding carried
out perhaps in the time of a short-lived Second Dynasty
of kings of whom even the names are unknown.

It was while we were clearing the back of the Ziggurat that we came upon something which tells not
of the glories of Ur but of its humiliation. Fallen to
the ground and lying on a brick pavement of very
late date there was a large diorite statue of a man
wearing the sheep-skin petticoat and bearing engraved

on his back and shoulders a long inscription giving his name, Entemena, king of Lagash, one of the cities which for a time held the hegemony of the valley and accounted themselves suzerains of Ur. The head was missing; it had been broken off deliberately in antiquity, and the jagged stump of the neck was polished as if by the contemptuous caresses of innumerable hands, and it is natural to suppose that the statue, set up by the overlord in his vassal city, had been mutilated and dishonoured by the inhabitants when for a space they regained their lost independence.

Entemena lived about 2750 B.C. and it is to this period that we may assign another object found preserved in the treasury of the temple of the Moon-goddess. This is a limestone slab carved in relief and perfectly preserved. There are two scenes upon it; in the upper a figure which, judging from its greater size, is probably that of the king, followed by the smaller figures of his sons, is pouring a libation in front of the statue of a seated god; in the lower the door of a shrine is represented, and in front of it a naked priest is making his libation, while behind him stands a woman in long garments and two attendants bearing offerings for the sacrifice. The scene is one of a series whose historical importance I shall describe later.

Of all the rulers who made themselves masters of Lower Mesopotamia in these troubled times of warring city-states the most famous was Sargon, a Semite who rebelled against his master and founded a new city of Agade or Akkad, which was to give its name to the whole North Country, so that 'King of Sumer and Akkad' became the regular title of the suzerain lord. For a long time it was supposed that he had no real historical existence, that under this fictitious name were grouped the deeds or the legends of a number of forgotten kings, and he was identified, perhaps rightly, with the Nimrod of the Old Testament who founded Caleh and was a mighty hunter before the Lord. Later documents were found which established the fact of his life and power, and now at Ur we have relics which add something to his history and illustrate the civilisation of his time.

Above the early cemetery of the prehistoric kings of Ur lie other graves, quite distinct from them, and distinguished by the difference of their contents. These belong to the time of Sargon of Akkad. The graves themselves are just like those of the early period, but the forms of the pottery are all new, and from the fact that much more care has been spent on their manufacture and that attention is paid to the appearance of the vessel, which might be covered with a wash of red paint and then brightly burnished, it may perhaps be argued that wealth was less than of old, for it is when men cannot afford cups and dishes of stone or metal that the humbler art of the potter comes into its own. Weapons, too, are very different; instead of the beautifully designed and admirably cast socketed axes of the older period, a clumsily shaped blade is simply hammered round the end of the wooden haft and made fast by a rivet; similarly the socketed arrow-head disappears, and is replaced by one with a tang which was driven into the shaft; everywhere there is less grace and inferior technique.

Fashions change in other things too; the old elaborate head-dress of the women with wreaths of gold leaves and gold hair-ribbons, and the man's head-band of gold chains and big beads of lapis lazuli and gold which kept the head-cloth in place, are found no longer; instead, an oval plate of the thinnest gold is tied across the forehead and two slender ribbons of gold are twisted spirally round two locks of hair which are brought from each side round over the brow and pinned one above the other.

We did find last winter one grave of this Sargonid age the riches of which recalled the great days of queen Shub-ad. It was a man's grave, and he wore not one but six of the oval gold frontlets on his head, heavy gold bracelets on his arms, gold finger-rings, quantities of beads, and with these had a gold amulet in the form of a standing goat very finely cast, and two lapis lazuli cylinder seals mounted in gold; he also wore a single gold ear-ring, which seems to have been the male fashion, since single ear-rings often occur in men's graves. But this was an exceptional case, so much so that it emphasised rather than redeemed the general character of the cemetery; one would not expect the graves of the inhabitants of a subject state to be very rich, and that the wealth of the First Dynasty was a thing of the past is shown perhaps most eloquently of all by the beads; stones unknown or rare in the old days, agate, chalcedony, and hæmatite, now become relatively common, but when gold is used we find only too often, instead of the solid metal, copper beads plated with the thinnest gold. In face of this it is not surprising that the city contains no great buildings of the age.

It would have been difficult to date the Sargonid cemetery but for one of those chances which, improbable as they may seem, do occur to help the archæologist. No less than three cylinder seals have been found, two of them actually in intact graves and one loose in the soil, bearing inscriptions in which there is added to the owner's name the statement that he held office in the household of the very daughter of king Sargon— one was her hairdresser, one her scribe, and one her steward. An object discovered in the ruins of the Moon-goddess's temple explains the otherwise unaccountable fact of the presence of Sargon's daughter at Ur; it is a disk of alabaster—the moon's disk—on one side of which is a much-damaged relief showing

a stepped altar, in front of which a priest is pouring
libations; behind the priest stands a female figure in
long flounced garments, and behind her two attendants
with offerings; on the back is a written dedication by
the daughter of Sargon.

Now, there is an inscription of Nabonidus, the last
of the kings of Babylon, describing how he appointed
his daughter High Priestess of the Moon-god at Ur,
and the king states that in so doing he was following
a precedent set by Kudur-Mabug, one of the Larsa
Kings, who had reigned some fifteen hundred years
before—about 2000 B.C. Clearly, long before Kudur-
Mabug's time, Sargon had done the same, and the
limestone slab of the period of Entemena, which was
been described above and bears precisely the same
scene rendered by a more primitive art, carries the
precedent further back still: all through history such
importance attached to the great Temple of Nannar
the Moon-god at Ur, and to the city as the main centre
of his worship, that the reigning king, though a foreigner,
might hold it worth his while to send his daughter as
High Priestess there; in one case at least a king's son
was High Priest of the Moon-goddess.

Not only then can we date our graves accurately—
king Sargon reigned from 2630 to 2575 B.C.—but we
can establish a new fact reflecting the glory of the
city even when it was not an imperial capital. It is
indeed a strange coincidence which has preserved from
a period so little represented in our excavations four
separate monuments all connected with one person,
and that the daughter of the outstanding figure of the
age.

CHAPTER IV

THE GREAT DAYS OF THE THIRD DYNASTY

AT no time in its long history was the City of Ur so important as in the days of the Third Dynasty, about 2300 B.C. to 2180 B.C., when it was the capital of the Sumerian empire. The founder of the dynasty was Ur-Nammu (or Ur-Engur, as the name used to be written), and he founded a royal house of which four generations after him were to sit upon the throne; he was a great conqueror and a great ruler, famous for his justice and his good works, whose dominions extended from the Persian Gulf to the Mediterranean, and his monuments were broadcast throughout the cities of Mesopotamia. It is a curious fact that no literary texts of his reign or of the reigns of his posterity survive, and that what we know of him has to be pieced together from scattered references and from the ruins of his buildings.

Two fragmentary inscriptions on stone found in the temple of the Moon-goddess throw some light on the beginnings of his kingdom. Each of them records the founding by Ur-Nammu of a temple or shrine, but whereas nearly all Ur-Nammu's other dedications are made to Nannar, the god of the city of Ur, here the deities he honours are the patron gods of the city of Erech, and he prays for the life of Utu-khegal the king of Erech, calling himself only by the title of 'governor.' Now, Erech was the seat of the dynasty which in the king-lists precedes that of Ur, and it is clear that when these temples were built Ur-Nammu was a vassal of Utu-khegal; it was by rebellion against his master that he made himself overlord of the empire.

When once he had established his position as independent king Ur-Nammu showed himself an indefatigable builder, but especially was he determined to make his own city worthy of its rank as capital. Probably during the long period of subjection to foreign kings and the comparative poverty which had resulted from that subjection the temples of the gods had fallen into disrepair; in any case, they were old and out of date: the programme of the new ruler provided for a virtual rebuilding of the whole central part of the city.

What strikes one most about the extant work of Ur-Nammu is its amazing solidity; he seemed to build for all time and shrank from no amount of labour to that end, and it is no wonder that his reign of eighteen years did not suffice for the completion of all he planned. Last winter we carried out some experimental work on the city walls and discovered the substructure of the defences with which Ur-Nammu encircled his capital. Rising 26 feet or more above the plain and acting as retaining-wall to the platform on which the town buildings were raised, there was a rampart constructed of unbaked brick throughout which at its base was no less than 77 feet thick! The wall proper, built of baked brick, which ran along the top of the rampart, has disappeared at the point where our trial excavations were made, but, judging from the unusually large size of the bricks employed for it, it must have been a very solid structure; but even apart from that, few kings would lightly embark on the task of putting up a wall 77 feet thick around a space which must measure some three-quarters of a mile in length and nearly half a mile in width, yet this was not the only work of Ur-Nammu and scarcely even the greatest.

About seventy-five years ago Mr. J. E. Taylor, then British Consul at Basra, was engaged by the British Museum to investigate some of the ancient sites of southern Mesopotamia, and amongst others he visited

Ur, in those days a place difficult and dangerous of access. Struck by the obvious importance of one mound, which from its height, overshadowing all the other ruins, he rightly judged to be the Ziggurat, he attacked it from above, cutting down into the brickwork of the four corners. The science of field archæology had not then been devised and the excavator's object was to find things that might enrich the cases of a museum, while the preservation of buildings on the spot was little considered. To the greatest monument of Ur Taylor did damage which we cannot but deplore to-day, but he succeeded in his purpose and at least made clear the importance of the site whose later excavation has so well repaid us. Hidden in the brickwork of the top stage of the tower he found, at each angle of it, cylinders of baked clay on which were long inscriptions giving the history of the building. The texts date from about 550 B.C., from the time of Nabonidus, the last of the kings of Babylon, and state that the tower, founded by Ur-Nammu and his son Dungi, but left unfinished by them and not completed by any later king, he had restored and finished. These inscriptions not only gave us the first information obtained about the Ziggurat itself, but identified the site, called by the Arabs al Mughair, the Mound of Pitch, as Ur 'of the Chaldees,' the biblical home of Abraham.

Taylor's excavations did not go very far. Those were the days when Rawlinson was unearthing in the north of Mesopotamia the colossal human-headed bulls and pictured wall-slabs which now enrich the British Museum, and dazzled by such discoveries people could not realise the value of the odds and ends which alone rewarded the explorer in the south: the site was deserted, and the upper stage of the Ziggurat which Taylor had exposed was left to the mercies of the weather and of Arab builders in search of cheap ready-made bricks, and when British troops advanced to Mughair in 1915 only a few bits of ragged brick showed at the corners of a mound up which a man could ride on horseback. In 1918 part of one end was cleared by Dr. Hall, and it was found that lower down the casing was wonderfully well preserved. In 1922–3 the excavation of the tower was seriously taken in hand and for two seasons employed a large number of our men, while work on the surrounding buildings was continued until 1929.

The amount of rubbish which had to be removed before the ruins of the tower stood free was very great, running into thousands of tons, and in all this mass we found scarcely any objects of interest. Near the surface of the lower part of the slope there were quantities of bricks covered with a bright blue glaze, wreckage from the little shrine with which Nabonidus had crowned the ancient monument; flung down in a gateway at the back of the tower we found the mutilated statue of Entemena to which reference has already been made, and in front of the tower fragments of an inscription on black stone, of late date, recording the buying-up of various blocks of house property for the enlargement of a temple; but otherwise we had to be content with the tower itself as the result of our prolonged toil. And it was a result well worth having. The top part, as we knew beforehand, was the work of Nabonidus, but the bulk of the construction was original, and on its bricks could be read the name and title of the first founder.

The Ziggurat is a peculiar feature of Sumerian architecture and as such calls for explanation. I have already said that we do not quite know who the Sumerians are; tradition would make them come from the East; the study of their bones and skulls shows that they were a branch of the Indo-European stock of the human race resembling what is called Caucasian man, a people who in stature and in appearance might pass as modern Europeans rather than as Orientals. Geographically,

it is likely that their original homeland was in hilly
country, and this is made more likely by certain facts
such as that their gods are often represented standing
upon mountains and the animals pictured in their art
are often of a mountain type, while the evidence that
their temple architecture was really a translation into
brick of an original timber structure would indicate
that they had first learnt to build in a wooded and
therefore in a high-lying country. People living in a
mountainous land nearly always associate their religion
with the outstanding natural features of that land and
worship their gods on 'high places,' and this would
seem to have been true of the Sumerians. When they
moved down into the alluvial plain of the Euphrates
they found themselves in a country where there were
no hills meet for the service of god, a country so flat
that even a private house, if it was to be safe from
the periodic inundations, had to be raised on an artificial
platform. The latter fact supplied a hint as to how the
former difficulty could be solved: the platform had
only to be built high enough, and there, made by man,
was the high place which nature had failed to provide;
and so the Sumerians set to work to build—using
'bricks instead of stone, and slime (bitumen) had they
for mortar'—a 'ziggurat' whose name might be called
'the Hill of Heaven' or 'the Mountain of God.' In
every important city there was at least one such tower
crowned by a sanctuary, the tower itself forming part
of a larger temple complex; of them all the biggest
and the most famous was the Ziggurat of Babylon,
which in Hebrew tradition became the Tower of Babel,
now entirely destroyed, but its ground-plan shows that
it was but a repetition on a larger scale of the Ziggurat
at Ur, the best-preserved of all these monuments.

The Ziggurat stands at the back of the temple of
Nannar the Moon-god, of which it is the main feature.
The outer court of the temple was a terrace raised 10

feet or more above the level in front of it, and behind
the court rose a second and higher terrace on which
stood the sanctuary and the tower. The tower measures
a little more than 200 feet in length by 150 feet in
width, and its original height was about 70 feet; the
whole thing is one solid mass of brickwork, the core
being of unbaked brick and the face a skin of baked
brick set in bitumen, about 8 feet thick. The walls,
relieved by shallow buttresses, are battered, or built
with a pronounced inward slope, and stand some 50
feet high; this forms the lowest stage. Above this point
the tower is taken up in steps or stages each smaller
than the one below, leaving narrow passages along the
main sides and wider terraces at either end; but the
stages are curiously unsymmetrical, so that there are
three storeys at the north-west end of the building
and four at the south-east end, all communicating by
flights of brick stairs; on the topmost storey, which
was virtually a square, stood the little shrine of the god.

On three sides the walls rose sheer to the level of the
first terrace (Plate IX *a*), but on the north-east face
fronting the Nannar temple was the approach to the
shrine. Three brick stairways, each of a hundred steps,
led upwards, one projecting out at right angles from
the building, two leaning against its wall, and all converging in a great gateway on the level of the second
terrace; from this gate a single flight of stairs ran
straight up to the door of the shrine, while lateral
passages with smaller flights of stairs gave access to
the terraces at either end of the tower; the angles
formed by the three main stairways were filled in with
solid flat-topped buttress-towers (Plate IX *b*).

When first we started the work of drawing out the
plan and elevations of the Ziggurat we were puzzled
to find that the different measurements never seemed
to agree; then it was discovered that in the whole
building there is not a single straight line, and that

what we had assumed to be such were in fact carefully
calculated curves. The walls not only slope inwards,
but the line from top to bottom is slightly convex;
on the ground plan the wall line from corner to corner
of the building has a distinct outward bend, so that
sighting along it one can only see as far as the centre;
the architect has aimed at an optical illusion which
the Greek builders of the Parthenon at Athens were
to achieve many centuries afterwards, the curves being
so slight as not to be apparent, yet enough to give to
the eye an appearance of strength where a straight
line might by contrast with the mass behind it have
seemed incurved and weak. The employment of such
a device does great credit to the builders of the twenty-
third century before Christ.

Indeed, the whole design of the building is a master-
piece. It would have been so easy to pile rectangle
of brickwork above rectangle, and the effect would
have been soulless and ugly; as it is, the heights of
the different stages are skilfully calculated, the slope
of the walls leads the eye upwards and inwards to the
centre, the sharper slope of the triple staircase accen-
tuates that of the walls and fixes the attention on the
shrine above, which was the religious focus of the whole
structure, while across these converging lines cut the
horizontal planes of the terraces, the division of the
building which they effect being emphasised by zones
of colour. At least in the later period the lower stages
were painted black, the uppermost was red, and the
shrine, as we have seen, was covered with blue-glazed
tiles, and it is probable that the shrine roof took the
form of a dome of gilded metal: these colours had
their mystical significance and stood for the various
divisions of the universe, the dark underworld, the
habitable earth, the heavens, and the sun.

No one looking at the Ziggurat can fail to notice
the tall and narrow slits which at regular intervals

and in rows one above another pierce the brickwork of the walls; they run clean through the burnt-brick casing and deep into the mud brick of the core, where they are loosely filled with broken pottery. These are 'weeper-holes' intended to drain the interior, a necessary precaution, for with damp the mud brick would swell and make the outer walls bulge if it did not burst them altogether.

This is the obvious and correct explanation and for a long time it satisfied us; but then the difficulty arose, how was the damp likely to get into the core? There was no real danger at the time of construction, for though there would then be plenty of water in the mud mortar used for the crude bricks, this would dry —indeed, with so vast an area to build over, one course would be virtually dry before the next was laid above it—and the tendency of the core would be to shrink rather than to expand. It is true that torrential rains fall in Mesopotamia, but in the days of the Third Dynasty it was usual to lay pavements of burnt brick two, three, or even five courses thick set in bitumen mortar, and no surface water could penetrate this and do harm below. If there had been such a pavement, the precaution was needless; and if there was not such, why not? And further, at each end of the tower there is in one of the buttresses a deep recess in the brickwork running from the edge of the first terrace to the ground, and at the bottom of this there is what engineers call an 'apron,' a mass of brick waterproofed with bitumen and built with its top at a slant calculated to carry off smoothly and without splash water falling from above: evidently there was water on the terrace.

In the doorway of a room of late date lying against the back wall of the tower we found the great diorite hinge-stone bearing an inscription of Nabonidus in which he refers to his repairs of the building and states that he cleared the 'Gig-par-ku' of fallen branches.

As the excavations progressed we were able to establish
that the Gig-par-ku was a part of the temple complex
dedicated to the Moon-goddess, and that it lay close
under the south-east end of the Ziggurat; somehow
the site of this building had become encumbered with
branches of trees. There may have been trees in the
Gig-par-ku itself, but as most of it was roofed in, this
is not very likely; and the only other place from which
the branches could have fallen into it was the Ziggurat
itself.

This explains the weeper-holes. The terraces of Ur-
Nammu's staged tower were not paved with brick but
were covered with soil, and in this trees were planted;
the long recesses in the buttresses may have carried
off the waters of a violent storm, but they may equally
have served as water-hoists for the irrigation of the
terrace; and what made possible the swelling of the
core of the tower and therefore necessitated the weeper-
holes in its facing was just this irrigation—the water
poured at the roots of the trees would percolate through
the top soil into the crude brick, and if it had no outlet
would really endanger the building.

Thus we have to imagine trees clothing every terrace
with greenery, hanging gardens which brought more
vividly to mind the original conception of the Ziggurat
as the Mountain of God, and we shall recognise how
much better the sloping outer walls harmonise with
this conception, rising as they do like the abrupt bare
sides of some pine-topped crag, than if they had been
uncompromisingly vertical, the walls of a house of man's
building.

With the destruction of the upper storey there is
nothing left to show the character of the shrine as
built by Ur-Nammu, but from what does remain we
can see how splendid a monument his Ziggurat was
and how well adapted for the use of those processions
which formed a part of Sumerian religious ritual; the

priests in robes of state bearing the statue and emblem of Nannar up and down the triple staircase against the background of coloured brick and trees must have made a magnificent spectacle, and it is easy to think that some tradition of these great feast-days was at the bottom of the vision which showed to Jacob ladders set up to Heaven and the angels ascending and descending on them. Yet the tower was only one part of the Temple of Nannar. Against one side of it lay the sanctuary of that temple, and in front of it, at a lower level, stretched the great court, a paved space some ninety yards across surrounded with chambers and store-rooms and entered by a triple gate passing under a high gate tower. The excavation of this has taken us a long time, and the temple had been so often altered and repaired that not much of the original founder's work survives, but its plan and a good deal of its history have come to light.

The walls which we first found when we came to dig deep along the confines of the temple were not those of the Third Dynasty at all; we got down to the foundations of the terrace and yet no sign of them appeared, and it looked as if they had been completely destroyed. Then it was found that a king reigning about three hundred years after Ur-Nammu had enlarged the terrace on which the court of the temple stands and had built a new retaining wall outside the old and, filling up the space between them with rubbish, had erected his new flanking chambers along the edge of the wider platform: we had to dig through the floors of these chambers to find the buried remains of the old terrace wall.

When it was found, a fresh problem arose: the lower section of the wall which supported the terrace was of mud bricks whose size proved them to be of Third Dynasty date, but they bore no stamp of authorship; such of the superstructure as was left, the walls of the range of rooms built along the terrace edge and enclosing the courtyard, were of burnt bricks stamped with the name not of Ur-Nammu but of his son Dungi. The bricks of the Ziggurat bear Ur-Nammu's name exclusively, the Ziggurat is part of the temple, and until the lower terrace of the courtyard was built the construction of the Ziggurat terrace and of the Ziggurat itself could not have been begun; therefore the mud-brick wall upholding the courtyard terrace must have been the work of Ur-Nammu. The inscribed cylinders of Nabonidus found by Taylor in the upper brickwork of the tower state that it was built by Ur-Nammu and his son Dungi; in the Ziggurat itself we have found no trace of Dungi's work, but since tower and temple are essentially one we can apply the statement to the whole building and see how well it harmonises with discovered facts.

Ur-Nammu started, as he was bound to do, with the substructures, the lower terrace which was to be the courtyard area, the higher terrace which was to be the platform for the temple sanctuary and the Ziggurat. As soon as that was done, he concentrated all his efforts on the sanctuary (where we find his brick-stamps commonly) and on the great tower, and so far as the evidence of the ruins goes he finished both these; then, before the walls of the outer court had risen above ground-level, the king died. Probably the early part of his reign of eighteen years had been spent in war, and during most of it he may have been absent from his capital and not so firmly established that he could afford to spend much time and money on bricks and mortar; certainly his building activity seems to have been confined rather to his later years and had been deferred too long; the temple of Nannar is not the only case at Ur where we have found the father's work completed by the son. In this case it was the outer court which Dungi had to build, and the fact of the divided authorship enables us to date the building with unusual precision—the scanty relics of burnt-brick construction which define the outlines of the court chambers belong to the very first years of the reign of the new king.

Very little of his work is preserved, and it would have been impossible to make out even its ground-plan but for the pious conservatism which Mesopotamian rulers observed in most of their dealings with temples; however thorough might be the repairs required, even though they amounted to the complete reconstruction of the fabric, the restorers were nearly always at pains to reproduce as nearly as might be the general lay-out of the old building. Very often they would raze the old walls but leave in position one course of bricks to serve as a guide to the new builders, and when such reconstruction has been repeated more than once we may find in the lowest four or five courses of the standing walls bricks stamped with the names of three or four kings of different dates, giving with each course a fresh chapter in the life-history of the temple. Here Dungi's walls had not been used as a substructure for the new building, but were buried uselessly beneath its floors, hacked away and cut across in every direction by the labourers who dug the trenches for the foundations of the larger temple, but just enough was preserved to prove that the new work did reproduce, though on a larger scale and in a more ornate form, the Third Dynasty model, and we could with full confidence complete on paper a plan which in the field was represented only by fragments of brickwork, shapeless and at first sight without meaning.

When we were clearing the ruins of the sanctuary lying under the shadow of the Ziggurat on its north-west side we found, re-used as hinge-sockets in a later doorway, two fragments of limestone carved in relief; in the courtyard of the temple Dublal-makh, some

hundred and fifty yards away to the south-east, more
carved fragments were discovered which actually fitted
on to the first two, and another piece apparently belonging to the same monument turned up in the ruins of
yet another temple, E-Nun-makh.

The fragments found thus widely scattered made up
a considerable part of a limestone stela which originally
measured 5 feet across and may have been as much
as 15 feet high. It was sculptured on both sides and
recorded in pictorial and in written form the achievements of Ur-Nammu. One scene at least commemorated
the king's exploits in war, for we have him seated
on his throne while prisoners with bound hands are
led before him; two scenes show sacrifice to the gods;
two panels, practically identical, are of a more unusual
sort—the king is represented standing in the attitude
of prayer, while an angel flying down from above pours
water on to the ground from a vase held between his
hands (Plate X a). An inscription giving a list of the
canals in the neighbourhood of Ur dug by orders of
the king explains the scene: Ur-Nammu has been responsible for the actual earth-work of the canals, but
he assigns to the gods credit for the blessed gift of
water which brings fertility to the land. It is a pleasing
instance of modesty in a great king, and the earliest
representation of an angel in art.

But there was another act of which Ur-Nammu
seems to have been particularly proud, seeing that to
it were devoted no less than three distinct panels of the
relief, and that is the construction of the Ziggurat.
In one scene the ruler is shown twice over making
libations, on the one side to Nannar and on the other
side to his wife the goddess Nin-Gal, and Nannar
holds out to him the measuring-rod and coiled line of
the architect, thereby symbolising his wish that Ur-
Nammu should build him a house (Plate X b). In the
next scene, sadly incomplete, the king obediently

presents himself before the god bearing on his shoulder
the tools of the architect and of the builder, compasses,
mortar-basket, pick and trowel; in a third, yet more
fragmentary, the workmen are seen carrying hods of
mortar up ladders and laying the bricks of the tower.
It is an extraordinary chance which has given us together
with the best preserved of all the ziggurats of Mesopotamia the contemporary record of its building, and
scarcely less extraordinary was the chance which brought
together fragments deliberately smashed and so widely
scattered. The monument is still very far from complete,
but at any moment we may discover fresh bits of what
is undoubtedly the most important sculpture known
from Ur.

The Ziggurat was itself so solidly built that we need
not be surprised if it stood almost unaltered and un-
repaired for seventeen hundred and fifty years, but the
Nannar Temple underwent in that time many changes.
In the courtyard we can trace various modifications,
some of which date from very little later than the time
of Dungi its joint founder: new altars were erected;
at one end there was built what seems to have been a
miniature ziggurat with a secret chamber hidden in
the heart of its brickwork; and then came the enlargement which has already been described. One feature
of the new temple deserves special mention, for it was
peculiar in itself and was to be copied by future restorers:
the outer façade and the wall dividing the court from
the sanctuary were decorated with brick half-columns,
down the centre of which ran double grooves or recesses;
this scheme of ornament, which belonged to the temple
standing in Abraham's time, is in striking contrast
to the normal Sumerian tradition of rectangles and
heavy masses almost unrelieved and must have given
to the building a grace quite new to the architects of Ur.

About six hundred years after this reconstruction
the temple of Nannar had become so ruinous that the

king who then reigned at Babylon and was overlord of the south country also razed its walls to the ground and built them afresh; for the outer façade he preferred a simpler style, plainly rectangular, but perhaps not less impressive; square buttresses with complicated re-entrant angles were set regularly along the front of the building with a deeper projection towards the centre, where there stood out boldly a huge gate-tower higher and more massive than that of former days; only inside the court the front wall of the sanctuary imitated with its rows of half-columns the work of six centuries before.

In about 650 B.C. fresh reconstruction was called for. During the preceding age various kings had carried out minor repairs, and we find new pavements of burnt brick laid down, the bricks stamped with the king's name, and old pavements patched with bricks nameless or borrowed from some other work; but now the governor who ruled Ur in the name of the king of Assyria was obliged by the state of the chief temple of the city to embark on a more thorough-going restoration. It is eloquent of the low estate on which Ur had fallen in these latter days that the Assyrian's work should have been of so shoddy a character; where he employed burnt bricks for wall foundations they were old material collected from the ruins, mere housebreakers' rubbish, and all his new buildings were in mud brick disguised by plaster and whitewash, while his floors were but of beaten mud.

When we started digging out the temple, the very first wall encountered was that of the Assyrian period dividing the court from the sanctuary, and at first it puzzled us not a little. Close below the modern surface a mud-brick wall was found and the pickman was ordered to follow it along; it ran straight for perhaps a yard, then took four right-angled turns in the length of a foot, then swelled out in a bold curve which after

x wall, by some nameless king of the Second
the old ziggurat was used by Ur-Nammu as
ion for his more ambitious building and either
:neath the level of his new terrace or, more
embedded in the core of his tower. It would
ne on our part to destroy one of the principal
nts of Iraq merely to prove the existence
we know must have existed, and the chance is
at we should find any such treasures as en-
ie platform of the temple at al 'Ubaid, which
fashion was buried beneath a new platform
King Dungi: here theory must suffice, for
never see the older Ziggurat of Ur.

cribing the temple I have more than once had
to mention the hinge-sockets of the doors,
phrase calls for explanation. The Sumerian
nsisted of a wooden leaf fixed to a pole rather
han itself; the top end of the pole was held
:tal ring projecting from the corner of the door
id revolved in it; the lower end was shod with
nd went down through a hole in the pavement
.nd turn on the hinge-stone. This was a boulder
rted hard stone, lime-stone or diorite, in which a
ped hollow had been cut to take the pole-shoe,
ierally one part of it (when the door was that
nple) had been smoothed and inscribed with the
f the king who dedicated the building and of the
whose honour he built it.

-sockets are thus invaluable evidence for the
nd nature of the buildings we unearth; they
be used with caution, because imported stones
aluable and an old socket would often be taken
nd re-used for some other building than that
ich it was first intended and the old inscription
o longer apply, but even so the text may yield
cts, and where the stone is certainly in its original
n the information it gives may be invaluable.

2 feet or so was broken by the eight angles of a double
recess and continued in a fresh curve back to the original
line, only to curve out again as before. The Workman,
hard put to it to distinguish the crumbling brick at all,
was further bewildered by these seemingly inconse-
quential meanderings of what ought to have been a
straight face, and reported that the wall was mad.
Mistrusting his work, for it is only too easy for a man
armed with a pick to carve the soft mud brick into a
shape quite other than that which the builder gave it,
I ordered him to retrace his steps and dig deeper to
a level at which the bricks might be better preserved;
he did so, and at a depth to which the rain-water did
not penetrate to rot the brickwork found the wall with
its coating of mud plaster and whitewash, pitted indeed
by the ravages of the white ant, but almost intact.

It was the wall built by Sin-balatsu-ikbi the Assyrian
more than 2,500 years ago, with its row of half-columns
and recesses copied from a model nearly 1,500 years
older still, and the whitewash was no worse than one
might see on any modern house in the nearest market-
town of Iraq; it was crumbly, and a touch would
flake it off, but it was the pride of our Arab pickmen
to use their tools so delicately that the columns freed
from the earth glistened white, and though the rains
of one winter washed away virtually every trace of
whitewash and mortar and reduced the sharp angles
and curves of the brickwork to a shapeless wavy line,
yet we have photographs in which the lower part of
the wall at least looks much as it did when the Assyrians
were masters of Ur.

One good reason for the wonderful preservation of
the whitewash was that the walls had not stood very
long above ground. Within fifty years of their being
built, the lower part of them had been protected by a
solid casing of earth. Nebuchadnezzar, who was king
of Babylon about 600 B.C., once more repaired the

Nannar temple, and part of his scheme was to bring the forecourt and the sanctuary to one level by raising the former; masses of soil were heaped over Sin-balatsu-ikbi's mud floor and a new brick pavement was laid down over this. Using the buried footing of the old walls as a foundation, he built new walls in mud brick with doorways at the new level, sank a well at one end of the court so as to have a handy supply of water for the temple rites, and then remodelled the sanctuary also, adding to it another wing on the south-east side of the Ziggurat and putting here a shrine which, judging from the long narrow brick base occupying the greater part of the chamber, was a 'boat shrine' containing the model of the ship in which the Moon-god crossed the sky—that high-prowed and high-sterned ship which is so like the moon's crescent.

This was the last transformation which the ancient temple was to undergo; no other royal builder interested himself in it, and before very long, when the Persian conquerors of Mesopotamia changed their religion and adopted Zoroastrianism with its worship of unembodied fire, Nannar's great house, like all the old temples, was doomed to destruction. Of Nebuchadnezzar's work very little survives to-day, only a few patches of brick pavement almost flush with the modern surface, a few bricks of the walls, and, deeper underground, the brick boxes which shelter the hinge-stones of the doors and prove by their position against the jambs of the buried doors of the Assyrian that Nebuchadnezzar's temple followed the lines of its predecessor: very little, but just enough to complete the life history of the most famous of the temples of Ur.

From the sixth century B.C. back to the twenty-third we have traced the evidence of reconstruction and repair and have laid bare what remains of the great building which Ur-Nammu planned and did not live to finish

but underneath that there
enough to prove that the T
the first to occupy the site,
it we shall never know m
found only a few bricks o
which goes back to the fourt
but when we were followin
temple enceinte which runs
form behind the Ziggurat,
evidence.

Inside Ur-Nammu's wall
ran underground, buried i
form, a wall of mud bric
though not quite of the ty
Dynasty of Ur, which were
and slantwise, herringbone fa
that this peculiar style of bu
between the First and the T
visionally we may assign it
of Ur about which in fact
The herringbone wall not on
but shows traces of cross-wall
chambers exactly like the chai
form-wall of Ur-Nammu and
earlier version of the same thi
the same purpose, i.e. it encl
stood a ziggurat and a temple

That there should have been
the days of Ur-Nammu is a f
so important a city as Ur could
from the earliest time, one of th
were typical of Sumerian arch
precisely where it stood. Un
of the Ziggurat which we see to
may remain of an older and a sm
ably as early as the reign of
repaired, as can be assumed fr

mud-bric
Dynasty,
a founda
buried t
probably
be a cri
monume
of what
slight tl
riched t
in like
built by
we shal

In de
occasio
and the
door cc
higher
by a m
lintel a
metal a
to rest
of impe
cup-sh
and ge
of a te
name
god in

Doo
date
have t
were
away
for w
may
new f
positi

Without such inscriptions it would have been impossible to identify the sanctuary of the Nannar temple and so to complete its ground-plan; we had not suspected its position and had no notion of the form it might assume, and the walls of the Ur-Nammu building were so terribly ruined, seldom standing at all above floor-level, that at first little could be made of them. The door-sockets lying below floor-level and therefore undisturbed bore the inscription 'the House of Nannar,' and from their position on the wall-line we could fix the whereabouts of the chamber doors, thus giving sense to the plan.

One furnished us with a new experience. The wall had vanished and only part of the bitumen-covered brick pavement was left, but in it was a square hole filled with earth; going down into this we found not only the block of diorite with Ur-Nammu's inscription but, still standing upright in the worn cup-like hollow in which it had once revolved, the copper shoe of the hinge-pole with a duplicate inscription on its side. The contrast between the complete destruction of the building above ground and the preservation of the hinge which had not even lost its balance on the stone could not but impress one.

At the far end of what we call the Sacred Area, the enclosure which contained the various buildings dedicated to the Moon-god or to the minor deities associated with him, there is another building of King Ur-Nammu. Part of this was excavated seventy years ago by Taylor, and where he dug very little of the structure survives to-day; another part was excavated by Dr. Hall, and the final clearing was done by the Joint Expedition. Dr. Hall found that the paved floors were of bricks stamped with the name of Dungi and giving the name of the buildings as 'the House of the Mountain,' apparently a palace. When we dug here we found that the bricks of the actual walls were stamped with

Ur-Nammu's name and the title of the building was merely 'the House of Nannar,' which might apply to almost any section of the Sacred Area.

Here there was a contradiction which had to be straightened out, so we searched the corners of the building for a 'foundation-deposit' and duly found what we had hoped for: built into the wall foundations at each corner there was a box of burnt bricks lined with matting and waterproofed with bitumen, and in each box there stood a copper object of which the upper half was a human figure from the waist upwards and the lower half more like a nail or cone; the figure was that of the royal founder presented in the guise of a temple servant or labourer bearing on his head a basket of mortar: in front of the figure there lay a small stone cut into the shape of a brick, the foundation-stone of the building. It was the regular custom at this period in Sumerian history to bury such statuettes and stones in the foundation-boxes, and the king's name and the name of the temple were recorded on the front of the figure and on the polished surface of the stone. What was, then, our dismay when, having looked to these very objects to solve all our difficulties, we found them absolutely blank! There was nothing to show whether the statuette represented Dungi or Ur-Nammu, whether the building were a palace or a temple. Then we had recourse to the doorways, and at every one we found a socket-stone in place, and not one bore a sign of inscription.

As the clearing of the building progressed its resemblance to the normal temple became more and more clear. At one end there was an entrance leading into a wide but shallow court from which a double gateway flanked by what seemed to be purification-chambers gave access to the main or inner court; on the far side of this two doors led through little antechambers into a long room which corresponded exactly with the sanctuary or Holy of Holies in other temples close by. A heavy wall running right through the building separated the 'temple' part from a complex of chambers clearly of a more domestic nature and divided into two apparently residential units each consisting of rooms grouped about an open central court; one of the groups was reached directly by a doorway from the inner court of the 'temple,' the other only by a winding passage and double doors from the 'sanctuary.' Most temples contained residential quarters for the priests, and therefore everything in the arrangement of this building agreed with its identification as a temple. But as against this there was the ambiguity of the texts on the bricks of the floor and the walls respectively, the uncompromising blankness of the foundation-figures, which ought to have been inscribed, and the equal blankness of the door-sockets—and we have never yet found a temple in which none of the door-stones bore an inscription. It was an archæological problem to which perhaps no final solution can be given, but one which the archæologist ought to do his best to solve so far as the evidence allows.

The contradiction in the question of authorship presents no great difficulty. The walls of a building must be put up before the floors are laid, and the two operations need not be the work of one person. Ur-Nammu built the walls and then died, leaving the building unfinished as he had left unfinished the Temple of Nannar, and his son Dungi put the final touches to it. Ur-Nammu calls it the 'House of Nannar,' which need mean no more than that it formed part of the group of religious foundations under the patronage of the god; Dungi may possibly have used for the floors bricks manufactured for another building whose site we have not yet discovered, but there is no need to assume this, and his name 'the House of the Mountain' may quite well be the particular name of the building

more vaguely described by his father. Copper foundation-figures such as we found in the corner boxes were,
so far as we know, only used for religious buildings,
but then they are generally inscribed, and the fact
that here they are not is against the building being
really a temple, and the same is true of the door-sockets.
The answer may be given by the ground-plan, which
is so like that of a temple that it almost proves the
building to be something else.

We know that according to Sumerian beliefs a king
was the vice-gerent of god upon earth—'tenant-farmer,'
they called him—and that the god was the real ruler
of the land. The god then being the king, his court
exactly reproduced that of his human representative.
Attached to the principal temple there would be ministers
of War and Justice, of Communications, of Agriculture,
of Finance, of the Harem, and so on; and as with the
personnel, so it was with the house in which the visible
statue of him was lodged: in the sanctuary he received
the adoration of those who might approach him, but
he also had his bed-chamber, his place for dining, and
necessarily, too, rooms and offices in which the business
of his temple and estates could be carried on. It is
most probable that in the details of its arrangements
a great temple, which was the House of God, afforded
a close parallel to the palace which was the house of
the king. We have many examples of temples and
none hitherto of palaces, but because Ur-Nammu's
building is so like a temple I think that we may accept
Dungi's name for it and take it to be the palace of the
kings of Ur.

If that be so, we might hazard an explanation of the
copper statuettes. The Sumerian kings claimed divine
powers and were deified in their lifetimes, so that the
royal palace would fittingly be placed within the Sacred
Area under Nannar's protection and its founding might
well be marked by the same ritual as that of a temple;

2 feet or so was broken by the eight angles of a double
recess and continued in a fresh curve back to the original
line, only to curve out again as before. The Workman,
hard put to it to distinguish the crumbling brick at all,
was further bewildered by these seemingly inconse-
quential meanderings of what ought to have been a
straight face, and reported that the wall was mad.
Mistrusting his work, for it is only too easy for a man
armed with a pick to carve the soft mud brick into a
shape quite other than that which the builder gave it,
I ordered him to retrace his steps and dig deeper to
a level at which the bricks might be better preserved;
he did so, and at a depth to which the rain-water did
not penetrate to rot the brickwork found the wall with
its coating of mud plaster and whitewash, pitted indeed
by the ravages of the white ant, but almost intact.

It was the wall built by Sin-balatsu-ikbi the Assyrian
more than 2,500 years ago, with its row of half-columns
and recesses copied from a model nearly 1,500 years
older still, and the whitewash was no worse than one
might see on any modern house in the nearest market-
town of Iraq; it was crumbly, and a touch would
flake it off, but it was the pride of our Arab pickmen
to use their tools so delicately that the columns freed
from the earth glistened white, and though the rains
of one winter washed away virtually every trace of
whitewash and mortar and reduced the sharp angles
and curves of the brickwork to a shapeless wavy line,
yet we have photographs in which the lower part of
the wall at least looks much as it did when the Assyrians
were masters of Ur.

One good reason for the wonderful preservation of
the whitewash was that the walls had not stood very
long above ground. Within fifty years of their being
built, the lower part of them had been protected by a
solid casing of earth. Nebuchadnezzar, who was king
of Babylon about 600 B.C., once more repaired the

Nannar temple, and part of his scheme was to bring the forecourt and the sanctuary to one level by raising the former; masses of soil were heaped over Sin-balatsu-ikbi's mud floor and a new brick pavement was laid down over this. Using the buried footing of the old walls as a foundation, he built new walls in mud brick with doorways at the new level, sank a well at one end of the court so as to have a handy supply of water for the temple rites, and then remodelled the sanctuary also, adding to it another wing on the south-east side of the Ziggurat and putting here a shrine which, judging from the long narrow brick base occupying the greater part of the chamber, was a 'boat shrine' containing the model of the ship in which the Moon-god crossed the sky—that high-prowed and high-sterned ship which is so like the moon's crescent.

This was the last transformation which the ancient temple was to undergo; no other royal builder inter-ested himself in it, and before very long, when the Persian conquerors of Mesopotamia changed their religion and adopted Zoroastrianism with its worship of unembodied fire, Nannar's great house, like all the old temples, was doomed to destruction. Of Nebu-chadnezzar's work very little survives to-day, only a few patches of brick pavement almost flush with the modern surface, a few bricks of the walls, and, deeper underground, the brick boxes which shelter the hinge-stones of the doors and prove by their position against the jambs of the buried doors of the Assyrian that Nebuchadnezzar's temple followed the lines of its predecessor: very little, but just enough to complete the life history of the most famous of the temples of Ur.

From the sixth century B.C. back to the twenty-third we have traced the evidence of reconstruction and repair and have laid bare what remains of the great building which Ur-Nammu planned and did not live to finish but underneath that there is still made soil and in it enough to prove that the Third Dynasty temple was not the first to occupy the site, though of what went before it we shall never know much. In the courtyard we found only a few bricks of that 'plano-convex' type which goes back to the fourth millennium before Christ; but when we were following up the back wall of the temple enceinte which runs along the edge of the platform behind the Ziggurat, we came on more decisive evidence.

Inside Ur-Nammu's wall and parallel with it there ran underground, buried in the filling of the platform, a wall of mud bricks, slightly round-topped, though not quite of the type of those of the First Dynasty of Ur, which were laid not flat but on edge and slantwise, herringbone fashion. Experience shows that this peculiar style of building belongs to a period between the First and the Third dynasties, and provisionally we may assign it to that Second Dynasty of Ur about which in fact we know nothing at all. The herringbone wall not only is parallel to the later but shows traces of cross-walls belonging to a range of chambers exactly like the chambers in the double platform-wall of Ur-Nammu and his successors; it is an earlier version of the same thing and it must have had the same purpose, i.e. it enclosed a terrace on which stood a ziggurat and a temple of Nannar.

That there should have been a ziggurat at Ur before the days of Ur-Nammu is a foregone conclusion, for so important a city as Ur could not have but possessed, from the earliest time, one of those staged towers which were typical of Sumerian architecture; now we know precisely where it stood. Underneath the vast bulk of the Ziggurat which we see to-day there lies whatever may remain of an older and a smaller tower: built probably as early as the reign of Mes-anni-pad-da and repaired, as can be assumed from the existence of the

D

mud-brick wall, by some nameless king of the Second
Dynasty, the old ziggurat was used by Ur-Nammu as
a foundation for his more ambitious building and either
buried beneath the level of his new terrace or, more
probably, embedded in the core of his tower.   It would
be a crime on our part to destroy one of the principal
monuments of Iraq merely to prove the existence
of what we know must have existed, and the chance is
slight that we should find any such treasures as enriched the platform of the temple at al 'Ubaid, which
in like fashion was buried beneath a new platform
built by King Dungi: here theory must suffice, for
we shall never see the older Ziggurat of Ur.

In describing the temple I have more than once had
occasion to mention the hinge-sockets of the doors,
and the phrase calls for explanation.   The Sumerian
door consisted of a wooden leaf fixed to a pole rather
higher than itself; the top end of the pole was held
by a metal ring projecting from the corner of the door
lintel and revolved in it; the lower end was shod with
metal and went down through a hole in the pavement
to rest and turn on the hinge-stone.   This was a boulder
of imported hard stone, lime-stone or diorite, in which a
cup-shaped hollow had been cut to take the pole-shoe,
and generally one part of it (when the door was that
of a temple) had been smoothed and inscribed with the
name of the king who dedicated the building and of the
god in whose honour he built it.

Door-sockets are thus invaluable evidence for the
date and nature of the buildings we unearth; they
have to be used with caution, because imported stones
were valuable and an old socket would often be taken
away and re-used for some other building than that
for which it was first intended and the old inscription
may no longer apply, but even so the text may yield
new facts, and where the stone is certainly in its original
position the information it gives may be invaluable.

Without such inscriptions it would have been impossible to identify the sanctuary of the Nannar temple and so to complete its ground-plan; we had not suspected its position and had no notion of the form it might assume, and the walls of the Ur-Nammu building were so terribly ruined, seldom standing at all above floor-level, that at first little could be made of them. The door-sockets lying below floor-level and therefore undisturbed bore the inscription 'the House of Nannar,' and from their position on the wall-line we could fix the whereabouts of the chamber doors, thus giving sense to the plan.

One furnished us with a new experience. The wall had vanished and only part of the bitumen-covered brick pavement was left, but in it was a square hole filled with earth; going down into this we found not only the block of diorite with Ur-Nammu's inscription but, still standing upright in the worn cup-like hollow in which it had once revolved, the copper shoe of the hinge-pole with a duplicate inscription on its side. The contrast between the complete destruction of the building above ground and the preservation of the hinge which had not even lost its balance on the stone could not but impress one.

At the far end of what we call the Sacred Area, the enclosure which contained the various buildings dedicated to the Moon-god or to the minor deities associated with him, there is another building of King Ur-Nammu. Part of this was excavated seventy years ago by Taylor, and where he dug very little of the structure survives to-day; another part was excavated by Dr. Hall, and the final clearing was done by the Joint Expedition. Dr. Hall found that the paved floors were of bricks stamped with the name of Dungi and giving the name of the buildings as 'the House of the Mountain,' apparently a palace. When we dug here we found that the bricks of the actual walls were stamped with

Ur-Nammu's name and the title of the building was merely 'the House of Nannar,' which might apply to almost any section of the Sacred Area.

Here there was a contradiction which had to be straightened out, so we searched the corners of the building for a 'foundation-deposit' and duly found what we had hoped for: built into the wall foundations at each corner there was a box of burnt bricks lined with matting and waterproofed with bitumen, and in each box there stood a copper object of which the upper half was a human figure from the waist upwards and the lower half more like a nail or cone; the figure was that of the royal founder presented in the guise of a temple servant or labourer bearing on his head a basket of mortar: in front of the figure there lay a small stone cut into the shape of a brick, the foundation-stone of the building. It was the regular custom at this period in Sumerian history to bury such statuettes and stones in the foundation-boxes, and the king's name and the name of the temple were recorded on the front of the figure and on the polished surface of the stone. What was, then, our dismay when, having looked to these very objects to solve all our difficulties, we found them absolutely blank! There was nothing to show whether the statuette represented Dungi or Ur-Nammu, whether the building were a palace or a temple. Then we had recourse to the doorways, and at every one we found a socket-stone in place, and not one bore a sign of inscription.

As the clearing of the building progressed its resemblance to the normal temple became more and more clear. At one end there was an entrance leading into a wide but shallow court from which a double gateway flanked by what seemed to be purification-chambers gave access to the main or inner court; on the far side of this two doors led through little antechambers into a long room which corresponded exactly with the

sanctuary or Holy of Holies in other temples close by.
A heavy wall running right through the building
separated the 'temple' part from a complex of chambers
clearly of a more domestic nature and divided into two
apparently residential units each consisting of rooms
grouped about an open central court; one of the groups
was reached directly by a doorway from the inner
court of the 'temple,' the other only by a winding
passage and double doors from the 'sanctuary.' Most
temples contained residential quarters for the priests,
and therefore everything in the arrangement of this
building agreed with its identification as a temple. But
as against this there was the ambiguity of the texts
on the bricks of the floor and the walls respectively,
the uncompromising blankness of the foundation-figures,
which ought to have been inscribed, and the equal
blankness of the door-sockets—and we have never
yet found a temple in which none of the door-stones
bore an inscription. It was an archæological problem
to which perhaps no final solution can be given, but
one which the archæologist ought to do his best to
solve so far as the evidence allows.

The contradiction in the question of authorship
presents no great difficulty. The walls of a building
must be put up before the floors are laid, and the two
operations need not be the work of one person. Ur-
Nammu built the walls and then died, leaving the
building unfinished as he had left unfinished the Temple
of Nannar, and his son Dungi put the final touches to
it. Ur-Nammu calls it the 'House of Nannar,' which
need mean no more than that it formed part of the
group of religious foundations under the patronage of
the god; Dungi may possibly have used for the floors
bricks manufactured for another building whose site
we have not yet discovered, but there is no need to
assume this, and his name 'the House of the Mountain'
may quite well be the particular name of the building

more vaguely described by his father. Copper foundation-figures such as we found in the corner boxes were,
so far as we know, only used for religious buildings,
but then they are generally inscribed, and the fact
that here they are not is against the building being
really a temple, and the same is true of the door-sockets.
The answer may be given by the ground-plan, which
is so like that of a temple that it almost proves the
building to be something else.

We know that according to Sumerian beliefs a king
was the vice-gerent of god upon earth—'tenant-farmer,'
they called him—and that the god was the real ruler
of the land. The god then being the king, his court
exactly reproduced that of his human representative.
Attached to the principal temple there would be ministers
of War and Justice, of Communications, of Agriculture,
of Finance, of the Harem, and so on; and as with the
personnel, so it was with the house in which the visible
statue of him was lodged: in the sanctuary he received
the adoration of those who might approach him, but
he also had his bed-chamber, his place for dining, and
necessarily, too, rooms and offices in which the business
of his temple and estates could be carried on. It is
most probable that in the details of its arrangements
a great temple, which was the House of God, afforded
a close parallel to the palace which was the house of
the king. We have many examples of temples and
none hitherto of palaces, but because Ur-Nammu's
building is so like a temple I think that we may accept
Dungi's name for it and take it to be the palace of the
kings of Ur.

If that be so, we might hazard an explanation of the
copper statuettes. The Sumerian kings claimed divine
powers and were deified in their lifetimes, so that the
royal palace would fittingly be placed within the Sacred
Area under Nannar's protection and its founding might
well be marked by the same ritual as that of a temple;

but where the building was in the king's own honour
there would be a difficulty about the inscription on his
statuette, and it might be omitted. We have never
found an inscribed door-socket in a private house, and
here the blank stone may mean that in Dungi's mind,
as his brick inscriptions show, the idea of the palace
of the earthly king overshadowed that of the house
of god's vice-gerent himself deified.

Certainly in this light we can interpret the building
satisfactorily. The temple-like section comprises the
public reception rooms where the ruler, seated on his
throne in the long back room, just like the god on his
pedestal in the sanctuary, gave audience to his subjects
gathered in the inner court; the two groups of residential
quarters were for the king and his women-folk respectively, and the difference between them agrees well
with this, one being easy of access, while the harem-
rooms are hidden away and hard to come to.

I have gone at length into this subject because the
interpretation of evidence is not the least important
part of the field-worker's task, and I have chosen a
problem to which the answer is not certain because
it illustrates better the kind of difficulty which one
encounters nearly every day and generally forgets as
soon as it is solved. If the identification of the building
which I have suggested is correct, it adds much to its
interest, for it is no small thing to possess the ruins
of the actual house of the greatest of the kings of Ur.

CHAPTER V

THE BUILDINGS OF THE LARSA KINGS

THE splendour of the Third Dynasty of Ur went out in shame and disaster. The sturdy mountaineers of Persia swept over the river-valley, the Sumerian forces were beaten in the field, the king of Ur was carried away captive, and when the Elamites returned to their hills they left behind them a wasted land with its temples overthrown and its cities in ruins. Ur, as the capital of the empire, must have borne the brunt of calamity and could not easily recover; when the Sumerians again lifted up their heads it was another city which took the lead, and the kings of Isin and Larsa, once vassal states, became in turn the overlords of Sumer.

But tradition was too strong for these 'foreign' rulers to neglect the old capital and the seat of the Moon-god's worship, and we find that not only were they active in repairing the damage wrought by the Elamites, so that most of the important buildings contain bricks stamped with the names of one or other of the Isin and Larsa kings, but the last king of Isin put his own son at Ur as high priest of the Moon-goddess Nin-Gal. This royal priest must have been something of a diplomat, for when his father lost his throne and the overlordship passed to the rival state of Larsa, he still managed to keep his position; that he also prospered in it is clear from the great buildings which he set up, but in his inscriptions he is careful to explain that these are offerings to the gods for the life of the Larsa king.

The temple of Nin-Gal had been built by Ur-Nammu's grandson, but it was only of crude mud brick and we may suppose that it had suffered much at the hands of the Elamite invaders; in any case, Enannatum the priest determined to rebuild it on the old lines but in better material. Excavating the site, we found his building standing on the stumps of the older walls which had been used by the new bricklayers as a foundation, and so recovered at one time the ground-plan of both temples.

The building was a rectangle measuring 240 feet either way, and was surrounded by an enormously heavy wall through the heart of which a narrow paved corridor ran round three sides of it, leading from a gate-tower over the main entrance to two fortified towers at the far corners; a similar corridor cut straight across the building, dividing it into two unequal parts and affording quick access from one tower to the other. From the outside at least the temple must have looked more like a military than a religious structure. Inside, however, its purpose was unmistakable. The larger section was again subdivided by a cross-wall, on one side of which was a complete temple lying just inside the main entrance and on the other minor shrines and living-quarters for the priests.

The temple, with its outer and inner court, its two little antechambers and its long shallow sanctuary, was identical in its arrangement with the audience-hall of Ur-Nammu's palace. At the same time it presented certain curious features. Between the outer and the inner court were two long chambers, of which the first had a wide doorway opening on to the outer court, and against the back wall, facing the door, a brick base for a statue; it looked as if this was a 'Court of the Gentiles' to which the general public would be admitted to pay their devotions before the statue in the half-way shrine, while the inner court was reserved for the priests. To reach this one passed through the second narrow chamber, round which ran a raised brick bench waterproofed with bitumen and having

along its edge a runnel for water; the floor also was
covered with bitumen and sloped gently to the door
leading to a tiny room in the centre of which was a
terra-cotta drain going deep down into the earth.
Obviously this was a lustral chamber, and here the
worshipper would purify himself before going farther
on to holy ground. The inner court and the sanctuary
had been terribly ruined, but enough remained of them
to show the place of the great altar of sacrifice in the
court and inside the sanctuary the bases of the statues,
the stepped altar, and the 'vestry' or treasury adjoining,
while behind the sanctuary was the long passage-like
chamber from which it is supposed that the priests
worked the oracle.

In all this part, and in the next section of the building,
excavation was made difficult by the presence of later
walls whose foundations went down nearly as deep as
the old work, while in some places the old floor-level
had actually been re-used and the new walls simply
set on the existing brick pavement. It was no easy
matter to unravel the tangle of ruinous brickwork and
to assign each fragment to its proper period, but when
this was done the early plan was found to be remarkably regular and what had seemed mere confusion
took on a very definite character.

The residential quarters of the priests were the most
ruined of all, for there had been here a motive for more
thorough-going destruction. In accordance with the
fashion of the time the priests had been buried beneath
the floors of their houses, and the brick vaults must
have contained riches which tempted the avarice of
the enemy who plundered the temple. In every case
the pavements had been dug up and the tombs broken
into and rifled so completely that there was scarcely
anything overlooked—indeed, the only object worth
mentioning which we found was a human face in
glazed frit. Interesting in itself as being one of the

earliest examples of polychrome glaze discovered in Mesopotamia, it was a tantalising sample of what the graves must once have contained, for the little statue from which it had been broken off was probably a rich and elaborate work of art.

Next to the living-quarters we found, very much better preserved, a building of a quite novel sort. From the corridor which ran through the temple precincts there opened off a narrow passage between blank walls with a door at the farther end; going through the door, one found oneself in a similar and parallel passage leading in the opposite direction, again with one door at the far end of the side wall; this took one across a narrow room and down two more passages back into the corridor: it was a regular little maze of which the long central room contained the secret. Standing between its two doors, one looked down the length of a chamber, now of course roofless and with un-decorated brick walls standing only some 5 feet high. The pavement was of brick, but the farther half of it was covered with bitumen on whose surface could be distinguished the impress of the reed mats which had once been spread there. Standing upright above the pavement, in which it was firmly bedded, was a large slab of white limestone, once round-topped, and side by side at its foot there lay fixed into the bitumen of the floor two other round-topped slabs of grey marble (Plate XI *a*), and on each of the three stones, in char-acters intentionally defaced but still legible, there was an inscription which read 'Bur-Sin king of Ur, king of Sumer and Akkad, king of the Four Quarters of the Earth, has built this to his lady Nin-Gal.' Against a side wall there was a low bench or table of bricks, and that was all.

What it meant was beyond doubt. The temple of the priest Enannatum reproduced exactly the older temple founded by Bur-Sin; in that there had been a little sanctuary set aside for the worship of the royal founder, who was also a god. When the Third Dynasty came to an end and the Elamites sacked Ur, they broke up the sanctuary and tried to erase the name of the king, but Enannatum, repairing the building, repaired the shrine also and set up once more the dishonoured stones. Probably a statue of the king was enthroned against the upright stone, and on either side of it would be set poles capped with the symbols of power, mace-heads and the heads of beasts; offerings would have their place on the brick table, and walls and floor would be gay with hangings and rugs; the pious would come down the winding passages and, pausing at the far end of the shrine, would pay their homage to the memory of the deified ruler. The shrine is dismantled now, of necessity, for the exposed ruins at Ur crumble in the rain and wind and are shrouded again in drifting sand; but the whole chamber has been reconstructed in the Museum at Baghdad, and stands there unique evidence of the divine honours paid to Sumerian kings.

The rest of the great four-square building beyond the cross corridor consisted of a second temple of a different pattern. From the main court three arched doorways led to the sanctuary, where the statue of the goddess set on a high brick base looked out to the court. All round and behind the sanctuary were service chambers and magazines devoted to various uses. In one a queerly-shaped pit sunk in the pavement puzzled us until modern analogy proved that it was a weaver's pit, wherein the weaver sits with his legs below floor-level while he works at his low loom. Another set of rooms formed the kitchen: in an open court there was a well, and by it a bitumen-proofed tank of water, and a big copper ring let into the pavement was for the rope, so that the bucket might not be lost down the well; against one wall were two fireplaces for boiling water, and against another the brick 'cutting-up table,' the criss-cross marks of the butcher's knife clearly visible on its top; in a side-room was the beehive-shaped oven for baking bread, and in another room the cooking-range with two furnaces and circular flues, and in the flat top of it rings of small holes where the cauldrons were to be set; after thirty-eight centuries one could yet light the fires and reconstruct with all its activities the oldest kitchen in the world.

But it was the sanctuary and the courtyard that gave us the best results. We had been a long time getting down to them, for close under the surface there were remains of the late Babylonian period which had to be planned and noted before they could be removed, and they were so fragmentary that we were hard put to it to make sense of them. The mud-brick walls had vanished and only broken pavements survived in patches, and it was hard to see where any one room began and ended. We had done our best and started to pull up the floors when a discovery was made which completed or confirmed the rather theoretical ground-plan we had evolved. Along every wall was a row of brick boxes placed immediately below the pavement, so that a pavement brick formed the lid of each; three bricks set on end made the box, whose fourth side, facing inwards to the room, was left open, and in each sentry-box stood a roughly modelled and painted figure of unbaked clay. There were snakes and dogs and gryphons, human figures and figures of men with the heads of lions or bulls, with bulls' legs or fishes' bodies, every sort of kindly demon that might guard the house and keep off sickness or ill-luck (Plate XIV a) and with each there was a bit of bone or a few calcined grains of barley, the relic of the feast that had been made when the guardians were put in their places. Cuneiform texts tell us about these figures and of the ceremony of their instalment with mystic formulæ and prayers; now we had actually found them still on duty, and they preserved for us at least the outline of the house.

Below this more shoddy buildings had to be removed, and then we came on a series of fairly massive mud-brick walls which proved to be those of a great house built probably for the temple priests in about 1400 B.C. with separate dwellings all giving on a central court. We were still high up in the mound, some 6 feet or more above the level of the pavements of Enannatum's temple, and this was a good sign. In this part of the building the walls, except for the open space of the courtyard, were close together, enclosing small chambers, and the walls were very thick; consequently when the upper parts of them were overthrown, the debris filled the rooms to a considerable height and the builders of the succeeding age could not be bothered to remove it; it was simpler to build on the top of the mounds and where the old court left a low-lying hollow to put in a flight of brick steps down to it. Thus we found the walls of the chambers round the sanctuary standing 6 feet high and the fallen rubble between them undisturbed, and as we went down through this we were delighted to come across a layer of ashes and burnt wood spread over the entire area.

Nothing helps an excavator like violent destruction. If a building has fallen slowly into decay, one can be sure that the impoverished inhabitants have removed everything of value. The best thing that can happen is a volcanic eruption which buries a place so deeply that nobody goes back to salve his belongings; but the ideal conditions of a Pompeii are seldom met with, and one must be thankful for smaller mercies. If an enemy sacks a temple or a town, he is sure to over-look some objects at least which were of small intrinsic value for him, but may be very precious for the archæo-logist; and if he was so considerate as to set fire to

the place and overthrow its walls, there is the
further probability that his search was hurried and
that no one else troubled to look for what he left
behind.

So it was here. The ashes represented the ceilings
and the panelling of the walls, and below them, lying
on the brick pavement, there were hundreds of fragments of alabaster and soapstone vases and splinters
of broken statues. One small statue we found entire,
a heavy and clumsy figure carved in black stone representing the goddess Bau seated on a throne supported
by geese; only her nose (which was made separately)
was missing, and round the head were the small drilled
holes to secure the gold crown which the robbers had
torn off before discarding the statue. Bau was the
patroness of the poultry farm, and this figure of her
in its flounced and pleated dress reaching to the ankles,
squat and thick-set, has an appropriately domestic
look; it is far from being a first-class work of art, but
as it is one of the very few Sumerian female statues
in the round which time has preserved to us, it must
rank high amongst our discoveries.

More fragmentary, for most of the head had vanished,
but it was of far finer work, was a little seated figure
of Nin-Gal herself, which bore a long inscription stating
that it had been dedicated by no less a person than the
priest Enannatum, the second founder of the temple.
This was pieced together from many fragments widely
scattered. As the splinters of stone were collected and
cleaned there began a regular jig-saw game, and it was
most exciting to watch them gradually growing up into
complete vessels, sometimes inscribed with the names
of ancient kings. A Sumerian temple, like a modern
cathedral, was a veritable museum of antiquities; for
centuries pious kings and others had been offering
their treasures for the service of the god, and the temple
strong-rooms would contain objects of all ages. It

was here that we found the alabaster lunar disk of
Sargon's daughter, and here too the limestone relief
showing sacrifice being done by a princess of much
older date—the latter was nearly a thousand years old
and the former seven hundred when the robbers broke
into the treasury where both were preserved.

One object was of peculiar interest. We found part
of a stone cup inscribed with a dedication by the
daughter of King Dungi, herself a high priestess of
the Moon-god; another cup fragment bore the name
of Sargon of Akkad, the great king who reigned 350
years before Dungi; and then it was found that the
two fragments joined together and that both inscriptions belonged to one and the same cup. How it came
about that the princess owned what had been so long
before the property of King Sargon we cannot tell,
but that she did so is another proof of the way in
which in the ancient as in the modern world objects
might long survive their generation: we shall see later
how another royal priestess of Ur indulged in a passion
for 'antiques.'

The stone fragments lay thickest in the neighbourhood of the sanctuary, but in the courtyard also they
were fairly abundant: at one end of this we found
bits, unfortunately not very numerous, of a large
alabaster slab inscribed with a list of the royal bene-
factions which had enriched the temple, and in the
middle of the court scanty remains of a much more
interesting document. There stood here a big base of
solid brick, and on it and round it we picked up pieces
of fine-grained black stone covered with inscription;
clearly the stone had originally been erected on the
base, and enough remained of the text to show that
it enumerated the conquests of the famous king and
law-giver, Hammurabi of Babylon, that Amraphael
who is mentioned in the fourteenth chapter of Genesis
as a contemporary of Abraham: Hammurabi reduced

Ur to subjection, and this was his war memorial set up in one of the chief temples of the city (Plate XI *b*).

Scattered at random in the chambers of the temple we found a number of inscribed clay tablets, part of the ordinary business records of the building. Such tablets are very often dated by the years of the reigning king, and on these we had represented most of the kings of Larsa, several years of Hammurabi, and the reign of his son almost continuously down to the eleventh year, and that was the last of the series. Now, the eleventh year was marked by a rebellion of the southern cities against Babylon, and the twelfth year was named 'that in which the king destroyed the walls of Ur'; here, then, we had a fixed date and a touch of drama. Ur had rebelled, and the destruction of Hammurabi's war memorial must have been an act of defiance on the part of the citizens; within twelve months, in the year 1885 B.C., so nearly as we can reckon it, the Babylonian troops burst into the city, looted Nin-Gal's temple, flinging away what it was not worth their while to carry off, and set it on fire; the challenge and its punishment were clearly written in the ruins.

It was not only the temple of Nin-Gal that suffered from the fury of the troops of Babylon; just outside the limits of the Sacred Area we excavated a section of the town proper, the residential quarter, and this too showed by its scorched walls and ash-covered floors that it had been overtaken at the same time by a like fate. It was one of the oldest parts of the city, where for many hundreds of years houses had been built and fallen into decay, only to pile up a platform for fresh building, so that by 2000 B.C. it was a hill rising high above the plain. Now the slopes were cut into terraces, and the houses of the time of Abraham stood on varying levels stepped down from the mound's summit to the flat ground below; when they were destroyed the uppermost might suffer severely, but those on the lower terraces were deeply buried by the rubbish fallen from above, and many were so well preserved that it was easy to picture them as having been deserted but yesterday instead of thirty-eight centuries ago.

The illusion was greatly helped by the method of digging which we adopted here, for instead of digging down from the top we dug from the bottom upwards. At the outset we encountered, high up, buildings of a later date, and being unwilling to destroy these without the justification of further discoveries awaiting us underneath, I made the workmen go down in certain spots between the walls of the late buildings to sound the deeper levels; 10 or 12 feet down we encountered walls which were built of burnt brick below—anything from five to fifteen courses of good brickwork set in mud mortar—and above of crude mud brick. These were good stout walls 2 feet thick; but whereas the burnt-brick footings were as true as when they were first built, the superstructure of mud brick had often been pushed out of the straight by the weight of the later buildings on top of them, and, since they no longer presented a vertical face, would be extremely difficult to trace if one came upon them from above. The workmen therefore were ordered to work at the bottom of their pits, following the burnt brick first, and only when its direction was certain clearing away the overhanging earth and exposing the face of the mud brick; where the mud brick had perished, as was often the case, the street or room was cleared, but the earth was left resting on the top of the burnt brickwork and gave the appearance of the wall which no longer existed. This, as I said, helped the illusion, but it was also an economical way of excavating, as it minimised the quantity of soil to be removed, and where a wall of the later period coincided with one of the earlier there was no need to destroy it in order to explore the earlier levels.

The houses excavated were private houses of middle-class rather than of wealthy citizens; they were of different sizes, and their ground-plan varied according to the exigencies of the available space and the means of the owner; but on the whole they conformed to one general plan. They had been plundered and burnt in 1885 B.C., and they had been built at any time between that date and 2100 B.C., most of them having been more than once restored or reconstructed, so that they gave quite definitely the type of dwelling belonging to a representative class during a fixed period (Plates XII and XIII a).

Judging from the private houses of the age of Nebu-chadnezzar which had been excavated by the Germans at Babylon, we had expected to find very modest dwellings one storey high and built of mud brick con-sisting of three or four rooms opening on to a court: instead of this we discovered that in Abraham's time men lived in houses built with walls of burnt brick below, rising in mud brick above, plaster and white-wash hiding the change in material, two storeys high, and containing as many as thirteen or fourteen rooms round a central paved court which supplied light and air to the house. The streets were narrow, winding, and unpaved, with on either side blank walls unbroken by any windows, streets such as one sees in any modern native town, impossible for wheeled traffic. Against one house a mounting-block showed that donkeys would be used for riding or for freight, and the corners of the narrow lanes were carefully rounded off to prevent injury to goods or riders.

Through the front door of a house one passed into a tiny lobby with a drain in its floor where the visitor might wash his hands or feet, and from that into the central court. On one side rose the brick stairs leading to the upper floor, and behind the stairs was a lavatory with its terra-cotta drain; then came the kitchen, distinguished by its fireplace and the stone grinders left on the ground; a reception-room with two doors or one door unusually wide was for guests, another room might be for the servants, and yet another the domestic chapel. Though the walls stood in some places as much as 10 feet high, there was no sign of ceiling-beams, so the ground-floor rooms must have been lofty, a great advantage in this hot climate. Of the upper floor nothing remained, and its existence had to be deduced from such evidence as was available.

In the first place, there was the staircase. It is true that the stairs might lead only to a flat roof, but it seemed unlikely that so much of the restricted ground space would be sacrificed to stairs serving no better purpose than that; the late houses at Babylon had flat roofs, but the only approach to them was by outside ladders, not by solid stairs; moreover, the use of the rooms on the ground-floor was tolerably certain, and there was no accommodation left for the family—there must therefore have been rooms above reserved for their living-quarters. The walls, internal and external alike, were so solid that it was natural to suppose that all rose to the full height of the house, so that the rooms above would duplicate those of the ground-floor, and in that case the access to them had to be considered. Below, all the chambers opened on to the court; above, a passage running round would have made the rooms impossibly small even if the floors would have stood the weight of a cross wall, which was unlikely, so that either they all opened out of each other or there was some other method of approach.

In the middle of each courtyard there was a drain to carry off water, and in one case part of the pavement had got into disrepair and a square patch of bricks had been laid round the drain-head on the top of the old pavement; this meant that the centre of the court was higher than the pavement nearer the walls, and water spilt on that surrounding part could never get to the drain, which therefore could not be intended to drain the court. Now, the roof of the house would be nearly flat, but sloping slightly inwards so as to carry off the rain-water, which would fall into the court, and its area was great enough for any ordinary storm to flood the court at once unless there were ready means of escape; the water could escape only if it fell not close to the house walls, but directly on to the raised pavement in which the drain was, and for this to be possible the roof had to project over the court considerably beyond the wall line. If this were so, the part of the yard which could not be drained would never get seriously wet. If the roof projected so much, it was presumably to shelter something, and the only possible thing was a gallery running round the court and giving access from the stair-head to the upper-rooms, whose doors in that case would correspond exactly to the doors on the ground-floor.

Examining the pavement carefully, we found that a single brick which was lying on it towards one corner was not there by accident but was bedded firmly in clay, and round it were remains of carbonised wood. The argument from this was clear. If the roof projected and if there were beneath it a gallery, there must have been corner posts for its support: given the character of the normal Eastern carpenter, one at least of the posts would be too short and would have to be jacked up on a brick or stone, and the brick actually found would be such a pole-rest and the burnt wood represented the pole. Restoring three other poles in corresponding places at the other corners, we found that we had a wooden gallery just 3 feet wide whose supports were conveniently arranged not to block any of the ground-floor doors. The staircase opened on to this,

and by its means one could go round to any of the
upper rooms without passing through the others. An
omen quoted on a contemporary tablet states that
'rooms opening out of each other are unlucky, but
those opening on to the court bring good luck,' and
our restoration exactly fulfilled the requirements of
superstition as well as of convenience.

We must revise considerably our ideas of the Hebrew
patriarch when we learn that his earlier years were
spent in such sophisticated surroundings; he was the
citizen of a great city and inherited the traditions of
an ancient and highly organised civilisation. The houses
themselves bespoke comfort and even luxury. Apart
from the actual fabric there was little left to throw
light on the daily life of the inhabitants, but one or two
stores of tablets did bear witness to their intellectual
interests. We found copies of the hymns which were
used in the service of the temples, and with them
mathematical tables ranging from plain sums in addition
to formulæ for the extraction of square and cube roots,
and other texts in which the writers had copied out
the old building inscriptions extant in the city and had
compiled in this way an abbreviated history of the
principal temples.

And another illuminating discovery was that of the
private chapels attached to the houses (Plate XIII b).
At one end of the room the pavement would be raised
by a single course of flooring-bricks, and on this there
would be built against the back wall a brick altar;
above the altar or at one side of it there would be a
shallow niche in the wall-face which was presumably
intended for the sacred picture or clay figurines of the
god, and against the side wall a square brick column
of uncertain use; under the 'nave' floor there would
be a vaulted brick tomb in which each member of the
family was laid when his turn came to die. Not every
house had a chapel, and where there was none the

family vault might lie under any room, and sometimes beneath the floors we found other single burials, the bodies set under inverted clay coffins shaped like baths. It was the custom that the dead man continued to inhabit the house in which he had lived and his heirs dwelt on in the rooms above his grave: the custom, barbarous as it may seem at first sight, accords with that feeling of family continuity which is so strong, for example, in the ancient Hebrews.

Occasionally we unearthed in the house ruins some of the small clay figures of which very many examples have been found in other parts of the residential site, figures representing gods and their worshippers. Sometimes they are rough models of the great temple statues, sometimes they seem to be of a more intimate sort; but where the statues in stone or precious metal have for the most part disappeared, these clay copies afford invaluable material for the study of contemporary art. They have a further interest in that they are the *teraphim*, the household images which Rachel stole from her father and Jacob buried under an oak in Shechem. They may have formed part of the furniture of the domestic chapels, and certainly they illustrate that more personal side of religion about which the texts concerned with the temple ritual have little or nothing to say.

One other aspect of life in the City of Abraham is brought into relief by our excavations. In the temple of Dublal-makh, about which more will be said later, there was found a hoard of many hundreds of tablets belonging to the business archives of the building. As king and landowner the god received rent and tithes and offerings of all sorts, and since there was no coined money, all these dues were paid in kind and required storage-room in the temple; hence the need of the magazines which surround every sanctuary. The Sumerians were essentially business-like, and no transaction was recognised in law unless it was witnessed to by a written document, and so for all incomings the priests drew up formal receipts of which copies were filed in the temple archives; whether it were a herd of sheep or a single cheese, a bale of wool or copper ore from foreign parts, the receipt was duly made out and entered. As the stores were drawn upon for the use of the temple, animals required for sacrifice, oil for squeaking door-hinges, wood for making a statue or gold for adorning it, the responsible official drew out an issue voucher giving the name of the recipient and his authority for the demand, and copies of these too were filed; a great hoard of these such as we found in Dublal-makh throws no little light on the secular activities of a religious house.

Further there were on the temple premises regular factories where the raw materials paid as tribute were manufactured into finished goods, and we have elaborate balance-sheets of such a factory in which women attached to the service of the god were employed in spinning wool and weaving cloth, balance-sheets drawn up every month and three months with a nominal roll of the workers, and, in parallel columns, the amount of raw wool each had received, the tally of her work and its cost reckoned by the issues made to her of food and supplies. It is all very practical and curiously modern, and again we see how very different from what we might have thought were the antecedents of the Hebrew people.

CHAPTER VI

THE MIDDLE AGE OF BABYLON

From the time of the destruction wrought by the Babylonians in 1885 B.C. darkness shrouds the city of Ur for nearly five hundred years. For the country as a whole it was not an exciting period; a succession of kings who are little more than names sat on the throne of Babylon and added nothing to its history. At Ur not a single monument bears witness to any one of them; so far as our excavations have gone, not one word of writing and not a brick in any of the buildings belongs to this stagnant age, and we can only suppose that the old buildings, patched up after the Babylonian inroad, were somehow sufficiently maintained not to make rebuilding imperative. At last, about 1400 B.C., there arose a king in Babylon, named Kuri-Galzu, who took an interest in the south country and thought it worth while to spend money in bricks and mortar: he started to repair the temples of the old Sumerian capital, but things had been allowed to go so far that his programme extended to a virtual reconstruction of at least the centre of the city.

The most striking monument of his that survives is the temple called Dublal-makh, the House of Tablets. Not far from the east corner of the Ziggurat there was a little low mound which we could identify as one into which Taylor had dug seventy years before and had found in it a two-roomed brick building with arched doors which he took to be a small house of late date. We cleared of the clean drift-sand the two rooms which Taylor's workmen had roofed in with mats, so high did the walls stand, and had used as a shelter for themselves, and then proceeded to lay bare the outer face. Of the brick arches over the two side doors which Taylor had noted, one had since fallen, but the other remained intact, and the bricks of doorway and of walls, good burnt bricks laid in bitumen mortar, were freely stamped with Kuri-Galzu's name and proved that this was no late building but a temple of the fourteenth century before Christ. The arch was by a thousand years the oldest example of an arch standing complete above ground, and though we have since found other arches older by nearly two thousand years, yet when the discovery was made in the winter of 1924 we could hail it as one which revolutionised the history of architecture.

Two more discoveries followed. First we found that though the building of burnt brick consisted of two small rooms only, yet it had been added to at a later period with walls of mud brick which with their decoration of vertical grooves imitated the older work, from which, thanks to a coat of plaster and whitewash applied to the whole, they were indistinguishable: about this addition I shall speak later. Then we found that the brick pavement which extended in front of the building belonged to the later period only; the walls of burnt brick went down deeper, and when we dug to their true ground-level this reached out only for 5 or 6 feet and then a fresh wall, grooved like that of the temple, dropped to a lower pavement. We followed this round and, cutting through the late brickwork and paved floor, exposed the original building, an isolated two-roomed shrine standing on a high pedestal which projected from the edge of the Ziggurat platform into a wide courtyard surrounded by high walls and chambers: this was the real Dublal-makh of Kuri-Galzu (Plate XIV b).

Of the little temple the antechamber was oblong in shape and had probably been vaulted; the inner shrine was square and, judging from the exaggerated thickness

of its walls, must have been roofed with a dome;
the outer door and that between the two rooms were
unusually wide and their jambs were elaborately adorned
with reveals, and since the smaller doors were arched
it can safely be assumed that they were arched also.
This would agree with the name of the building as
inscribed on the bricks of the doorway; instead of
'The House of Tablets' we find here written 'The Great
Gate'; and when seven hundred and fifty years later
the temple was restored by the Assyrians, it was the
'gate' that was most emphasised. We found a door-
socket of beautiful green stone bearing a long inscription, in which the governor of the city, after describing
the dilapidation of the old building, boasts that he
restored the Great Gate and set up doors of box-wood
overlaid with brass, having silver hinges and lock-
plates of gold. Why one and the same temple should
possess two different names was not obvious until
further excavations solved the problem in a very interesting way.

Most of the brick pavement inside the ante-chamber
had been destroyed by Taylor's workmen, and we
therefore could dig down below floor-level without
doing further damage. Just where the floor had been,
the character of the bricks in the walls changed slightly,
and stamped upon them was the name not of Kuri-
Galzu but of a king of Isin who had reigned seven
hundred years before him; and the walls went down
to the level of the outer court. Working on the outer
face of the building where the pedestal had fallen
away, we found that while the containing wall of the
latter was Kuri-Galzu's work, the filling consisted of
broken bricks of the Isin period, and instead of running
under the walls of the temple proper it only ran up
against them; in short, the pedestal was not what it
appeared to be, a substructure on which the temple
was built, but a skin masking the base of its walls;

and the masked portion was older than the superstructure.

Now things became clear. Kuri-Galzu had found the
Isin temple ruinous and even its foundations giving
away: he had razed the walls down to a height of
about 6 feet from the ground, built a fresh wall round
them, and had filled in the space between the old and
new walls, and the interior of the chambers, so as to
make one solid block; then on the stumps of the old
walls, now flush with his platform surface, he had
built a temple which was an exact replica of its predecessor; even the grooves on the wall-face reproduced
the decoration of the time of the Isin king. But this
older temple was not the first to occupy the site: under
its walls we found others, rather differently aligned,
stamped with the name of Bur-Sin, king of Ur in the
Third Dynasty, and at the back was mud brickwork,
part of it of the same Third Dynasty period—about
2220 B.C.—and part of it built in the herringbone style
with round-topped bricks and going back some hundreds
of years more to the Second Dynasty. The Second
Dynasty brickwork was a relic of the great ring-wall
which enclosed the Ziggurat terrace, and since that
line never altered, the back of Dublal-makh was always
flush with or embedded in the terrace wall.

Examining the temple again in the light of this knowledge, we could see that its own back wall was not
original but an after-thought—it was a blocking of
what had once been an opening; and the oldest floor
surviving in the sanctuary, that of Bur-Sin, was not
flat but was stepped up from the antechamber so as to
bridge the difference of levels between the low-lying
outer court and the Ziggurat terrace. Originally the
building had been the gateway of the Ziggurat, 'The
Great Gate.' The foundation-inscription of Bur-Sin
found on a door-socket further helped us; the building
had been roofless and ruinous, and he had repaired

and covered it in and had made it 'his Court of Justice, the net from which the enemies of Bur-Sin shall not escape.' That was the last clue required.

The original building was the gateway to the Ziggurat, and since by it one passed on to holy ground, the particular precinct of the Moon-god, it was itself holy, and in the inner gatechamber there would almost certainly be put a statue or an altar to which one could pay reverence on entering; from a gate to a gateway shrine is but a natural transition. By the immemorial custom of the East the judge 'sits in the gate to give judgment,' and already by the time of Bur-Sin the Ziggurat gate had by its special sanctity come to be regarded as the king's supreme court. A remodelling of the Ziggurat platform and the making of a new entrance to it did away with the *raison d'être* of Dublalmakh, and the door to the terrace was blocked up and the building became simply a two-roomed temple.

But just as the name Ludgate has survived the walls of London, so tradition preserved the old name of the Great Gate, and even when Kuri-Galzu restored it in the fourteenth century B.C., this was the title inscribed by him on its door-jambs. The court still sat here, and its findings, written on clay tablets, were stored in the temple archives to be consulted in future cases, and from the new pedestal, standing under the huge arched doorway with the statue of the god in his shrine visible in the background as the inspirer and ratifier of judgment, the judges would pronounce their sentence to the crowd assembled in the broad paved court below.

Nearly always the inscriptions of Kuri-Galzu begin with a set formula, 'that which was fallen down and of old time ruined from its foundations he has rebuilt,' making no claim to originality. He restored Dublalmakh, he restored the great temple of Nannar, as has been described, and the smaller temple of Nannar and his wife, the building called E-Nun-makh. There is only one striking exception to the ru'e. Of the temple of Nin-Gal set up by the royal priest Enannatum, the north-western half he did as usual restore, so far as the small temple in it was concerned, but the rest of the building was too ruinous and too deeply buried. Here he abandoned the old plan, and over the mounds covering the south-eastern temple set up houses for the lodging of the priests. But since Nin-Gal for some reason or other required twin shrines, Kuri-Galzu founded a new one inside the Ziggurat enclave on ground which had hitherto stood open, and here his inscriptions give him full credit as the first builder. It is interesting to see that here, where he had a free hand, the king adopts a plan unlike that of any of the older temples. There is an outer court with buildings round it, but the sanctuary complex, the temple proper, forms an isolated block, a small square compact building divided into a number of narrow chambers all once vaulted while over the central chamber rose a dome: it is exactly in the line of descent of modern Arab architecture.

Kuri-Galzu not only founded a temple here, but started a tradition. To unearth his building we had to dig through two temples of later dates set in the same place and dedicated to the same goddess. By 650 B.C. the Babylonian building was ruined and buried in its ruins, and the Assyrian governor who was commissioned to restore the sacred buildings of Ur had to start his work afresh and at a higher level. A hundred years later Nabonidus, last of the independent kings of Babylon, re-floored this temple and added to it a new and more imposing entrance, on the strength of such alterations claiming it as his own construction.

The reconstructed building was in a very ruinous state and contained few features of interest, but that of Sin-balatsu-ikbi the Assyrian proved more fruitful. One feature was distinctly novel. In the courtyard he did which was entirely new. The old Sacred Area had consisted of religious foundations of all sorts grouped together and in theory forming a unity, but the unity was ill-defined; sometimes the outer walls of adjacent temples were continuous, sometimes the buildings were more loosely disposed, and it would seem that in fact the Sacred Area in many places merged imperceptibly into the lay quarters of the town. Nebuchadnezzar reformed all this. A space 400 yards long and 200 yards wide was marked out, a rough rectangle which enclosed all the important buildings of Nannar's enclave, and round this was built a wall of mud brick. It was a double wall with chambers in the middle of it, the flat roofs of which would make a broad passage along the wall-top available for the manœuvring of troops in its defence; it was 33 feet wide and probably about 30 feet high, the face of it was decorated with the double vertical grooves which were traditional for temple walls (Plate XV *a*), and it was pierced by gateways of which six have been discovered; the main gate, with a high gate-tower set back in a deep recess, led immediately to the entrance of Nannar's chief temple.

Parts of this great Temenos Wall are well preserved and stand 6 feet high and more, and in other parts where it ran over high ground and was therefore more exposed it was difficult to trace it. We have not dug it right out all the way round—that would teach us no more than we know and would only mean the total destruction of the mud brick by rain and wind—but having excavated carefully certain sections, we traced the rest by means of shallow trenches which revealed only the upper courses, and so were able to complete the entire circuit of the Temenos in eight days. Sometimes in the course of tracing we were temporarily baffled by unexpected changes in direction, and it is indeed difficult to explain the minor irregularities in the line taken by the wall. In places, where the back of an old temple projected outside the area pegged out, it has been ruthlessly cut away, and the wall of enclosure makes the new back wall of the building; elsewhere the line is deflected as if to enclose some monument which had to be respected, but as only too often the denudation of the surface has resulted in the complete disappearance of the monument we cannot accept the explanation as certain.

Possibly there was a simpler reason. Examination of the wall proves that it was built by various gangs of workmen each having his own section, and the collaboration between them was not very good in that the foundations of adjoining sections are laid at different levels and the projecting footings are not continuous; the irregularities of line may be due merely to faulty methods.

But the Temenos Wall was an imposing structure, and with its completion the Sacred Area took on a new character; it was much more a place set apart than it had been in the past. And inside the wall nearly everything bore the stamp of Nebuchadnezzar's creation. To-day over a good half of the enclosure the weathering of the mounds has left no vestige of the Late Babylonian buildings, and in other places there may remain no more than such scarcely intelligible wreckage as I described in connection with the clay figures of guardian gods found under the pavement; but from what survives one can safely argue that Nebuchadnezzar left very little untouched. We have seen that he remodelled the great temple of Nannar and raised the level of its outer court; a description of the temple called E-Nun-makh will illustrate his radical treatment of old buildings.

The very first building which we excavated at Ur was E-Nun-makh. A low hillock rising close to the Ziggurat mound seemed to promise good results, and a trench driven into its flank at once produced walls of burnt brick enclosing paved chambers. It was a small square five-roomed building; the door led into an antechamber against the back wall of which, facing the entrance, was a brick base for a statue, and four doors, two in the back wall and one at either end, gave access to the other rooms which ran back the depth of the building. The two inner rooms were an exact pair; each had a bench near the door and was divided into two parts by a screen; in the farther part there was a brick altar against the wall and in front of it a brick table; obviously each was a shrine for religious services. The two outer rooms were also a pair, but here there were no particular features to show their use. The duplicating of the arrangements in the temple was explained by the inscriptions on the bricks: it was the common shrine of Nannar and his consort Nin-Gal, and in it each deity had his or her special sanctuary.

In front of the building stretched a brick pavement half enclosed by two projecting wings which had been added in mud brick to the original square of the shrine; immediately in front of the door stood an oblong brick altar for offerings, and to one side remains of a second and larger altar from which a covered drain led right across in front of the temple door to some exit beyond the court; the pavement extended only to the line of the frontage of the mud-brick wings and was then stepped down to a lower level and continued to a boundary-wall which separated it from the Sacred Way running through the Sacred Area (Plate XV b).

The bricks of the pavement bore no stamp of authorship, but their size and character proved them to be Persian, belonging to the very latest date in the history of Ur, and as a gate in the Temenos Wall close by had been restored by Cyrus the Great, we can probably attribute to him the last reconstruction of the temple also. It was interesting to observe that the position of the building and the details of its arrangement agreed almost exactly with the description which Herodotus gives of the great temple at Babylon in Persian times, but subsequent discoveries were to prove more interesting still.

It was clear that though the floors were Persian the walls of the shrine were very much older; in the outer court there was an earlier pavement visible where the new had been broken through, and the same might be true of the chambers also. The order was given to test this by pulling up twelve bricks in one of the sanctuaries and digging down beneath them. Our Arabs, who were [new to the work, and had always been told that on no account must they disturb any brick that was in place, could not understand this sudden sacrilege, and when they found the order was serious jumped to the conclusion that we were looking for buried gold, nor would they believe me when I said that what we wanted was a second brick pavement. I went off, leaving the men at work, but within a few minutes one of them came running to fetch me. 'We have found the gold!' he said, and sure enough just below the paving-slabs there was a whole treasure of gold beads and ear-rings and pendants and one long gold pin topped with a little figure of a woman wearing a long dress. It might have been a votive deposit; more probably the things had been buried there for safety in some moment of peril and had been forgotten. Nothing of the kind was found anywhere else in the room or in the other rooms of the temple, and nothing would convince the Arabs that we had chosen to lift those twelve bricks without knowing what lay beneath them.

Fortunately, the second pavement was there as well as the gold, and about one in every four of its bricks bore the long stamp of Nebuchadnezzar, and this lower floor reproduced in every particular that of the Persian period: there were the same benches, altars, and tables, and in the court outside the same altar in front of the door; only the second altar and the drain were missing, but the level between the wings of the building dropped as before to the wide outer court which reached to the temple walls.

The outer court was in bad condition, much of the pavement gone, and what remained curiously irregular, all in ridges and hollows. The reason for this was obvious from the outset and was proved as the work was carried down deeper: it had been laid over a series of chambers, and where the floor rested on the wall-tops it kept its level and where it had beneath it only the rubbish with which the old rooms were filled it had sunk or broken up altogether (Plate XV *b*). In the upper courses of the walls we found brick-stamps of Kuri-Galzu, and his socket-stones were in position by the doors, but fairly high up in the rubbish; in 1400 B.C., therefore, the rooms had been in use and had been restored with mud floors which lay only a very little below the pavement of Nebuchadnezzar, but they had been built earlier than that.

Lower in the walls came bricks of one of the Larsa kings (his floor had vanished), showing a previous reconstruction; and then we found, mixed with the rubbish filling of the chambers, innumerable fragments of stone vases, some of them bearing inscriptions with the names of kings going back almost as early as the time of Sargon of Akkad (his own son was amongst them) and coming down to the close of the Third Dynasty of Ur. The vases belonged to a temple treasury and must have been broken up when Ur was sacked by an enemy, and judging from the dates given by the inscriptions, the occasion would have been the Elamite disaster which brought to an end the Third Dynasty, when the city of Ur was looted and burnt; afterwards the scattered fragments of the sacred vessels must have been gathered up by some pious person and given decent burial under the new floor of E-Nun-makh.

Still the walls went down, and now we found on their bricks the stamp of Bur-Sin, king of the Third Dynasty, and below them mud bricks which we should scarcely have been able to identify but for the fact that in one place there was a vertical drain running through the wall to carry off rain-water from the roof, and this was constructed with burnt bricks and bitumen and bore the name of Ur-Nammu, the founder of the royal house: he had built the temple in mud brick and his grandson had rebuilt it in more lasting material. Nor was Ur-Nammu the first to build: under his walls there were broken fragments of a construction in the round-topped mud bricks of an earlier day, and under these again walls of yet a more primitive description, built with what one could scarcely call bricks at all, so shapeless were they, mere lumps of clay which had been brought still damp and soft and set in clay mortar hardly to be distinguished from themselves, so that the whole 'green-walling' structure, as our Arabs named it, having been like rude work in modern times, became a homogeneous mass resembling *terre pisée* rather than a builded wall.

The temple was indefinitely old. Too little was left of the earliest building to show its form, but from the days of Ur-Nammu at least up to and after those of Kuri-Galzu, that is for more than a thousand years, successive builders had respected and repeated its ground-plan. The small five-chambered sanctuary was a thing apart; it lay at the back of the building and was reached only by a passage which ran round three of its sides; on the other side of the passage there were store-rooms and priests' chambers occupying the whole of the rest of the temple area and completely masking the sanctuary—it was hidden away and made as difficult of access as might be. I have said that the sanctuary rooms were very small and would hold but few people at a time; taking this in conjunction with its inaccessibility, we are driven to conclude that E-Nun-makh was designed for a secret ritual such as might be fitting in what was really a harem temple, the special quarters of the god as married: only the priests would enter here and in privacy wait upon the twin deities.

This ancient tradition was completely set at naught by Nebuchadnezzar. when he restored the temple. The rooms in front of the sanctuary, store-rooms and rooms which, as tablets found in them showed, were for the priestesses specially dedicated as concubines of the god who would naturally be at home in this harem building, were swept away; the whole front of the sanctuary was opened up; where the passage had been there was a raised pavement in the centre of which an altar rose, a statue-base was erected in the antechamber of the sanctuary facing its door, and where had been a maze of chambers the wide lower court afforded accommodation for a crowd of spectators. In the old temple everything had been secret; now a numerous public could watch the priest making his offerings on the open-air altar and behind him could see through the dim sanctuary's open door the image of the god.

There is no doubt that the remodelling of the building implies such a change of ritual, but how can this itself be explained? The answer is given by the Old Testament story of the Three Children in the Book of Daniel. However miraculous a tale may be, its setting must have a certain verisimilitude, must contain some element of truth. Now, the gist of the story is this, that Nebuchadnezzar made a great image and set it up in a public place and ordered that at a given signal everybody was to fall down and worship it; the Jews, who seem to have lived hitherto undisturbed in the land of their captivity, were by this order given the choice between idolatry and disobedience involving death. What was

there new in the king's act? Not the setting up of a
statue, because each king in turn had done the same;
the novelty was the command for general worship by
the public: for a ritual performed by priests the king is
substituting a form of congregational worship which all
his subjects are obliged to attend. So striking is the
correspondence between the written story and the facts
of the ruins and so completely do they explain each
other that we must needs accept the background of
the legend as historical. The alterations in E-Nun-
makh were designed deliberately with a view to the
religious reform attributed to its builder by the Old
Testament.

Another old building was to undergo in these latter
days a transformation not less radical. I have described
Dublal-makh and its many vicissitudes down to the time
when the Assyrian governor in 650 B.C. made its gates
splendid with silver and gold; what I did not say was
that in spite of his boasts the governor carried out most
of his restorations with very poor material—the walls
were of crude mud brick and the floor of beaten mud—
and that what he did soon fell into disrepair. A hundred
years later the work was again taken in hand by Nabonidus, the last of the Babylonian kings, and when we excavated the site his were the buildings which we first
encountered.

In 550 B.C. nearly 8 feet of accumulated rubbish buried
the court and surrounding chambers of the old temple,
and no attempt was made by Nabonidus's workmen to
clear them; instead the ground was levelled and new
buildings were erected without any reference to what
lay below: only the two-roomed shrine, the real Dublal-
makh, raised high on the pedestal which had been
built round it 850 years before, still stood above ground
and could be incorporated in the new temple. On either
side of the shrine new rooms were added whose walls,
decorated with vertical grooves and covered with plaster

and whitewash, could not be distinguished from the old; one of these was a kitchen, one a room for ablutions with a bench for washing-basins and a drain, and one, with a doorway as imposing as that of the original shrine, must have been a second sanctuary. Flush with the threshold of the great gate there extended a large open court paved with brick and surrounded by buildings. Those which actually fronted on the court opened on to it and did not communicate with each other; they were for the most part fairly large, and one would judge them to be intended for the official business of the temple. But facing the sanctuary entrance at the far end of the courtyard was a wide gateway from which a passage led right through to the rear of the building, and opening off this there were small complexes, each consisting of an open court with chambers along one or two sides of it, which were manifestly separate private residences, though as all lay within the heavy enclosure wall of the temple they were an essential part of the latter. To explain this there were brick inscriptions in plenty. Nabonidus was the builder; the building was dedicated to the Moon-goddess; it was a nunnery for the priestesses attached to the worship of Nannar and his spouse.

Now, from the inscriptions found seventy years ago by Taylor, we know that Nabonidus installed as High Priestess at Ur his own daughter, giving her much good advice as to her conduct in the post, and his new building, the E-gig-par as he called it, was to be her house. The old sanctuary of Dublal-makh presumably served as a sort of private chapel for the sisterhood, who, or at least the principal of them, were lodged in the separate quarters at the far end of the building, and the largest of these may well have been reserved for the princess herself, Bel-Shalti-Nannar, the sister of that Belshazzar who is notorious in Bible story.

The nunnery was interesting not only for its plan and associations, but also for its contents. In front of one of the side doors of the antechamber of Dublal-makh there lay a round-topped limestone relief on which was represented the god Ea, patron deity of the ancient city of Eridu whose ruins break the line of the horizon some twelve miles to the south-west of Ur. According to the old Sumerian convention the god is shown holding a vase from which two streams of water are pouring to the ground, while fish are swimming up and down in the streams; as lord of the Waters of the Abyss Ea holds the source from which rise the twin rivers Tigris and Euphrates, givers of life to the land of Mesopotamia. The relief may have decorated the space above the door, but if so it was re-used, for it has nothing really to do with this Late Babylonian building but is a product of the great art of the Third Dynasty: how an object seventeen hundred years older than the nunnery came to be lying on its threshold will become evident from what follows.

Another object, found this time by the door of the kitchen which Nabonidus added to the sanctuary, was certainly of contemporary date, but it again was a stranger to its surroundings. Crushed together under a fallen brick we found at least a hundred slithers of ivory, many of them minute in size and as thin as tissue-paper, the ivory having rotted and split into its natural laminations: so delicate were they that they had to be hardened with celluloid before they could be picked up from the ground. When put together, the fragments took shape as a circular toilet-box decorated with figures of dancing girls carved on it in relief; Egyptian rather than Oriental in style, the row of maidens hold hands and make a ring around the casket. This box was never made in Mesopotamia; it is the work of one of those Phœnician craftsmen of Sidon or of Tyre whose skill in ivory-carving had made them famous throughout the Mediterranean world; as an imported object it must have been a thing of price—indeed, that it was valued is clear, for it had been broken and riveted in antiquity—and possibly it belonged to the princess Bel-Shalti-Nannar herself.

But it was when we were clearing the surroundings of the courtyard that the discovery was made which most threw light on the character of the king's daughter. In a very much ruined room whose mud-brick walls rose scarcely above pavement level, one of the rooms fronting on the court which we had taken to be the business offices of the temple, we found a number of clay tablets of what are called the 'school exercise' type; they are flat disks of clay used for the teaching of writing. On one side the master inscribed his 'fair copy,' some easy sentence often taken from a well-known text, and the tablet was then handed to the scholar, who, after studying it, turned it over and on the back tried to reproduce what he had read; sometimes the copy is very faulty and sometimes the boy has made a second attempt on the same tablet. We found a number of these, and with them broken fragments of other 'school' texts, bits of syllabaries giving columns of words all beginning with the same syllable, much like an old-fashioned English spelling-book, and one fragment of a dictionary on which was an endorsement 'the property of the boys' class.' Here was definite proof that the priestesses kept a school on their premises.

And a still more up-to-date touch was given by the contents of the next room. The pavement was very close to the modern surface, which was terribly denuded by weather, and not more than a foot of loose rubbish covered the brickwork; there seemed little hope of finding anything in such a spot. But suddenly the workmen brought to light a large oval-topped black stone (Plate XVIa) whose top was covered with carvings in relief and its sides with inscriptions; it was a boundary-stone recording the position and the outlines of a landed property, with a statement as to how it came legally into the owner's hands and a terrific curse on whosoever should remove his neighbour's landmark or deface or destroy the record. Now, this stone belonged to the Kassite period of about 1400 B.C. Almost touching it was a fragment of a diorite statue, a bit of the arm of a human figure on which was an inscription, and the fragment had been carefully trimmed so as to make it look neat and to preserve the writing; and the name on the statue was that of Dungi, who was king of Ur in 2280 B.C. Then came a clay foundation-cone of a Larsa king of about 2000 B.C., then a few clay tablets of about the same date, and a large votive stone mace-head which was uninscribed but may well have been more ancient by five hundred years.

What were we to think? Here were half a dozen diverse objects found lying on an unbroken brick pavement of the sixth century B.C., yet the newest of them was seven hundred years older than the pavement and the earliest perhaps two thousand: the evidence was altogether against their having got there by accident, and the trimming of the statue-inscription had a curious air of purpose.

Then we found the key. A little way apart lay a small drum-shaped clay object (Plate XVI*b*) on which were four columns of writing; the first three columns were in the old Sumerian language, and the contents of one at least were familiar to us, for we had found it on bricks of Bur-Sin, king of Ur in 2220 B.C., and the other two were fairly similar; the fourth column was in the late Semitic speech. 'These,' it said, 'are copies from bricks found in the ruins of Ur, the work of Bur-Sin king of Ur, which while searching for the ground-plan [of the temple] the Governor of Ur found, and I saw and wrote out for the marvel of beholders.' The scribe, alas! was not so learned as he wished to appear, for his copies are so full of blunders as to be almost unintelligible, but he had doubtless done his best, and he certainly had given us the explanation we wanted. The Room was a museum of local antiquities maintained by the princess Bel-Shalti-Nannar (who in this took after her father, a keen archæologist), and in the collection was this clay drum, the earliest museum label known, drawn up a hundred years before and kept, presumably together with the original bricks, as a record of the first scientific excavations at Ur.

Before long the storm which had long been gathering in the East burst. Belshazzar, who had been acting as regent for his father and commanded the troops in the field, was defeated and killed by the invading Persian army; Nabonidus was taken prisoner when Babylon fell, and his dominions passed into the hands of Cyrus the Great. Cyrus seems to have paved the way for his armed attack by a campaign of scurrilous propaganda directed against the person and character of the late king, and after his victory he took a particular pleasure in defacing his monuments; at Ur the ruinous state of Nabonidus's buildings is often manifestly due to wilful vandalism. But the conqueror was not so secure on his newly-won throne that he could afford to flout the feelings of his subjects, and a definite policy of conciliation provided for the repair of the temples, even of those which had been desecrated as being memorials of the last independent king.

When we were tracing the course of the great Temenos Wall built by Nebuchadnezzar we found in one of the north-east gates the stone door-sockets in position in the brick boxes which kept the earth away from the hinge, and the bricks bore the inscription of Cyrus; the new ruler had repaired the circuit wall of Nannar's temple, and, as we have seen, it was almost certainly he who was responsible for the last restoration of E-Nun-makh, the joint shrine of Nannar and Nin-Gal. The inscription on the bricks has a familiar ring; 'the great gods have delivered all the lands into my hand,' it begins, and we think of the proclamation of Cyrus in the Book of Ezra which also had to do with the restoration of a temple: 'The Lord God of Heaven hath given me all the kingdoms of the earth; and he hath charged me to build him an house at Jerusalem, which is in Judah.' That act of clemency, which to the captive Jews appeared miraculous, was an incident in a scheme applied to the whole kingdom: whether the god was Jehovah or Nannar mattered little to Cyrus; his purpose was to placate his people by subsidising their particular forms of worship, and the temples of Ur gained a fresh lease of life from the catholic generosity of the Persian.

But the lease was a short one. The city had long since lost all political importance and deserved consideration only as a traditional centre of religious feeling in the South, and it was perhaps about this time that an event occurred which was to seal its doom for ever. In the old days the river Euphrates, or an important branch of the river, washed the walls of Ur on the west, and from it innumerable canals big and small led the water off into the fields which spread far across the plain, and up and down the main canals went the ships bringing trade from the Persian Gulf and from the other towns on the river-banks. To-day the Euphrates runs 10 miles to the east of the ruins and the great plain is a barren desert. When the river changed its course we do not yet know, but the drying-up of the old bed meant the stoppage of water-borne traffic, the ruin of the whole elaborate system of irrigation, and the end of agriculture; there was not the energy or the capital for the installation of a new system, and the starving city had no longer any reason for existence. Gradually the inhabitants moved away to other homes, the houses crumbled, the winds sweeping across the now parched and desiccated levels brought clouds of sand which they dropped under the lee of the standing walls, and what had been a great city became a wilderness of brick-littered mounds rising from the waste.

It is very likely that the blow fell in the Persian period. After Cyrus no king's name appears on any brick to show that the government was at all interested in the buildings of the city; on the contrary, all the evidence proves that neglect speedily brought them to ruin. In the rubbish heaps which covered the sanctuary of Nannar's great temple we found crooked walls ill built of old bricks collected from ruins of all dates; they were mere huts without symmetry or plan, but under the foundations we discovered a clay jar containing tablets which proved that this was the last degenerate phase of the temple. Here a handful of priests lived on and eked out their existence on the tithes which a faithful few still brought to the dishonoured House of Nannar.

On the other side of the Ziggurat we unearthed, lying above the chambers built by Nabonidus for the service of Nin-Gal's temple, kilns set up by some Persian potter; his ovens ran up almost against the side of the huge tower, and the 'wasters,' the pots damaged in the firing, and the little clay tripods which kept apart the plates piled in the kiln and prevented the glaze sticking them one to another, were mixed in the rubbish with the blue-glazed bricks fallen from the walls of the little shrine which was the Ziggurat's crowning glory. Here and there in the remains of Persian houses dated tablets have been found which carry on the history of the inhabited town to about the middle of the fifth century before Christ, and thereafter there is silence.

About this time the Persian kings definitely adopted the Zoroastrian creed, whose pure monotheism rejected the images and temples of idolatry, and very likely iconoclasm hastened at Ur the slower process of natural decay; but that process of itself was sure. The populous city became a heap, its very name was forgotten; in the holes of the Ziggurat owls made their nests and jackals found a hiding-place, and the Bedouin pitched their camps under the shelter of the 'Mound of Pitch,' little guessing that here had lived Abraham, the founder of the Jewish nation and of their own race, Ibrahim Khalil Abdurrahman, the Friend of God.

INDEX

INDEX

PENGUIN BOOKS

COMPLETE LIST OF PUBLICATIONS TO APRIL, 1938

FICTION   *orange covers*

FICTION (continued)

73 MR. WESTON'S GOOD WINE by T. F. Powys
75 DECLINE AND FALL by Evelyn Waugh
76 DANGEROUS AGES by Rose Macaulay
80 THE DAWN OF RECKONING by James Hilton
81 TARKA THE OTTER by Henry Williamson
83 THE POACHER by H. E. Bates
84 LOLLY WILLOWES by Sylvia Townsend Warner
85 SIR ISUMBRAS AT THE FORD by D. K. Broster
86 THESE CHARMING PEOPLE by Michael Arlen
87 GREENERY STREET by Denis Mackail
88 THE GREEN LACQUER PAVILION by Helen Beauclerk
91 GHOST STORIES OF AN ANTIQUARY by M. R. James
92 THE HAMPDENSHIRE WONDER by J. D. Beresford
93 WILD STRAWBERRIES by Angela Thirkell
94 SATURDAY NIGHT AT THE GREYHOUND by John Hampson
95 THE MAN WHO WAS THURSDAY by G. K. Chesterton
96 SELECTED MODERN SHORT STORIES selected by Alan Steele
97 SOME EXPERIENCES OF AN IRISH R.M. by Somerville and Ross
102 YOUTH RIDES OUT by Beatrice Kean Seymour
103 A TALL SHIP by "Bartimeus"
104 DEEP WATERS by W. W. Jacobs
105 MANTRAP by Sinclair Lewis
106 NOW EAST, NOW WEST by Susan Ertz
107 PRIVATE WORLDS by Phyllis Bottome
108 KAI LUNG UNROLLS HIS MAT by Ernest Bramah
109 THE FIDDLER by Sarah Gertrude Millin
112 CHILDREN OF THE EARTH by Ethel Mannin
120 PENGUIN PARADE (I)—New Stories
121-2 LEAN MEN by Ralph Bates (in two volumes)
123 SOLDIERS' PAY by William Faulkner
125 AN INDIAN DAY by Edward Thompson
132 MR. PERRIN AND MR. TRAILL by Hugh Walpole

FICTION (continued)

CRIME FICTION *green covers*

TRAVEL & ADVENTURE *cerise covers*

TRAVEL & ADVENTURE (continued)

67 MY SOUTH SEA ISLAND by Eric Muspratt
68 WITH MYSTICS AND MAGICIANS IN TIBET by Alexandra David-Neel
69 } SOME EXPERIENCES OF A NEW GUINEA RESIDENT
70 } MAGISTRATE by C. A. W. Monckton (in two volumes)
82 UNDERTONES OF WAR by Edmund Blunden
99 } THE WORST JOURNEY IN THE WORLD : ANTARCTIC
100 } 1910–1913 by Apsley Cherry-Garrard (in two volumes)
113 THE SECRET OF THE SAHARA by Rosita Forbes
126 TRADER HORN by Alfred Aloysius Horn
133 WATKINS' LAST EXPEDITION by F. Spencer Chapman
139 FLYING DUTCHMAN by Anthony Fokker

BIOGRAPHY & MEMOIRS dark blue covers

1 ARIEL by André Maurois
7 TWENTY-FIVE by Beverley Nichols
29–30 AUTOBIOGRAPHY by Margot Asquith
71 CONFESSIONS AND IMPRESSIONS by Ethel Mannin
77 GREY WOLF : MUSTAFA KEMAL by H. C. Armstrong
110 DISRAELI by André Maurois
114–115 FOCH : MAN OF ORLEANS by B. H. Liddell Hart
128 LORD OF ARABIA: IBN SAUD by H. C. Armstrong

MISCELLANEOUS yellow covers

116 ON ENGLAND by Stanley Baldwin
118 WHILE ROME BURNS by Alexander Woollcott
119 BILLIARDS AND SNOOKER FOR AMATEUR PLAYERS by Horace Lindrum
129–130 THE WEEK-END BOOK (in two volumes)

DRAMA red covers

117 SEVEN FAMOUS ONE-ACT PLAYS

PENGUIN SPECIALS

S1 GERMANY PUTS THE CLOCK BACK by Edgar Mowrer
S2 BLACKMAIL OR WAR by Geneviève Tabouis
S3 MUSSOLINI'S ROMAN EMPIRE by G. T. Garratt

THE PENGUIN SHAKESPEARE
Specially edited for Penguin Books by Dr. G. B. Harrison.

B 1	TWELFTH NIGHT	B 10	ROMEO AND JULIET
B 2	HAMLET	B 11	JULIUS CAESAR
B 3	HENRY THE FIFTH	B 12	MACBETH
B 4	KING LEAR	B 13	HENRY IV, part i
B 5	AS YOU LIKE IT	B 14	HENRY IV, part ii
B 6	A MIDSUMMER NIGHT'S DREAM	B 15	MUCH ADO ABOUT NOTHING
B 7	THE TEMPEST	B 16	OTHELLO
B 8	THE MERCHANT OF VENICE	B 17	ANTONY AND CLEOPATRA
B 9	RICHARD II	B 18	THE SONNETS

Other volumes to follow shortly.

PELICAN BOOKS *light blue covers*

A series of books on science, economics, history, sociology, archæology, etc. Edited by V. K. Krishna Menon ;—*advisory editors* : H. L. Beales, Reader in Economic History, University of London ; W. E. Williams, Secretary, the British Institute of Adult Education ; Sir Peter Chalmers-Mitchell, Secretary of the Zoological Society, London, 1903–35.

A 1 }
A 2 } THE INTELLIGENT WOMAN'S GUIDE TO SOCIALISM, CAPITALISM, SOVIETISM AND FASCISM by Bernard Shaw (in two volumes)

A 3 LAST AND FIRST MEN by Olaf Stapledon

A 4 DIGGING UP THE PAST by Sir Leonard Woolley (*with 32 half-tone plates*)

A 5 A SHORT HISTORY OF THE WORLD by H. G. Wells (*with numerous maps*)

A 6 PRACTICAL ECONOMICS by G. D. H. Cole (*first publication*)

A 7 ESSAYS IN POPULAR SCIENCE by Julian Huxley (*illustrated*)

A 8 THE FLOATING REPUBLIC by Dobrée and Manwaring (*The mutinies at the Nore and Spithead in 1797*)

A 9 A HISTORY OF THE ENGLISH PEOPLE (I) by Elie Halévy

PELICAN BOOKS (continued)

More volumes to follow.

N.B.

New volumes are continually being added to Penguin and Pelican Books. Please ask your bookseller for the latest list, as further volumes may have been issued since this book was printed. Suggestions of books for inclusion in the series are always welcome.

PELMANISM

PELMANISM is a system of training the mind on scientific lines. It has sometimes been described as "Psychology made popular and practical," but it is something more than that. The system is taught through the medium of fifteen "little grey books" which are accompanied by examination papers. After studying the first of these books, the student answers the accompanying examination paper to the best of his or her ability, and this paper is sent up to an examiner, who marks it and adds appropriate comments. Then the second book is taken, and so the Course continues until the fifteen lessons are completed.

A course of Pelmanism brings out the mind's latent powers and develops them to the highest point of efficiency. It banishes such weaknesses and defects as:

Depression	Mind-Wandering	Weakness of Will
Unnecessary Fears	"Inferiority Complex"	Procrastination
Indefiniteness	Pessimism	Forgetfulness

which interfere with the effective working powers of the mind, and in their place it develops strong, positive, vital qualities such as:

—Optimism	—Will-Power	—Reliability
—Concentration	—Tact	—Decision
—Judgment	—Initiative	—Self-Confidence

By developing these qualities Pelmanism certainly adds to your Efficiency and consequently to your Earning Power.

But what is equally important, Pelmanism increases your happiness and enables you to develop a finer appreciation of the beauties of Nature, the Arts, and Life generally. In a sentence, Pelmanism enables you to live a fuller, richer, happier and more successful existence.

"The Science of Success"—Free

The Pelman System is fully explained in a little book entitled "The Science of Success." The Course is simple and interesting and takes up very little time, and, you can enrol on the most convenient terms. The book will be sent post free on application to-day to—

Pelman Institute

(Established 40 years)

252 Pelman House, Bloomsbury Street, London W.C.1.

PELMAN (OVERSEAS) INSTITUTES : PARIS, 80 Boulevard Haussmann. NEW YORK : 271 North Avenue, New Rochelle. MELBOURNE, 396 Flinders Lane. JOHANNESBURG, P.O. Box 4928. DURBAN, Natal Bank Chambers (P.O. Box 1489). DELHI, 10 Alipore Road. CALCUTTA, 102 Clive Street. AMSTERDAM, Damrak, 68. JAVA, Malabarweg, Malang.